D1148366

SUPERVISI
AND LEADERSHIP
IN TOURISM AND HOSPITALITY

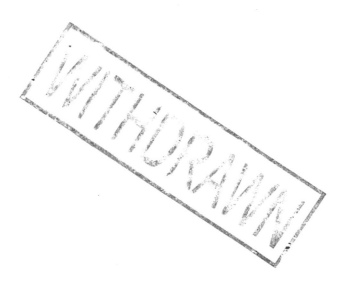

SUPERVISION
AND LEADERSHIP

IN TOURISM AND HOSPITALITY

LYNN VAN DER WAGEN AND CHRISTINE DAVIES

CASSELL

Cassell
Wellington House
125 Strand
London
WC2R OBB

First published by Hospitality Press, 1998

British Library Cataloguing-in-Publication Data
A catalogue record for this book is available from the British Library.

ISBN 0-304-70686-8

Edited and produced by Bridging the Gap: Publishing & Marketing, Sydney
Design concept by Bowra + Bowra, Sydney
Design by Eckermann Art & Design, Sydney
Cover and text illustrations by Maria Miranda, Sydney
Printed in Australia by Quill Graphics Pty Ltd, Melbourne, Victoria

contents

introduction

A number of indicators suggest that career opportunities for tourism and hospitality supervisors are outstanding. There is also evidence to show that there is likely to be a shortage of trained staff in the industry at this level. One of the reasons for this could be the large number of relatively unskilled casuals employed in the tourism and hospitality industry who are generally not interested in, or qualified for, promotion. Tourism Workforce 2020 (Tourism Training Australia, 1996) predicted that by 2000 an additional 7,100 managing supervisors would be required for the hospitality industry (restaurant, catering, accommodation and tavern). With continuing growth in all service sectors, this industry is likely to display steady growth even beyond the year 2000.

A career in hospitality has only become popular over the last decade or so as the importance of the tourism and hospitality sector has been recognised. International tourism and travel is one of the world's largest industries. The World Travel and Tourism Council estimated that in 1995 the industry contributed around 10.9 per cent to world Gross Domestic Product (GDP) and employed around 10.7 per cent of all employees. It makes a vital contribution to the economies of many countries by providing employment, foreign exchange earnings and economic growth.

International tourism contributes significantly to the Australian economy. The tourism industry (including domestic tourism) accounted for approximately 6.6 per cent of GDP in 1993–94. Inbound tourism contributed about 1.8 per cent to GDP in the same year. And tourism accounts for nearly 7 per cent of the workforce.

In 1995–96 international tourism to Australia generated export earnings of $14.1 billion, accounting for more than 12.8 per cent of Australia's total export earnings and 63.1 per cent of services exports.

There is a significant gap in skills and knowledge between operative level and supervisory level staff in the tourism and hospitality industry. While operative staff need to follow routine procedures, supervisory staff need to monitor, amongst other things, unexpected events, such as higher than predicted levels of business. Planning and organising for such contingencies is part of the supervisory role. There are, in fact, many challenges associated with work at supervisory level, given the dynamic nature of the industry and the demands of the individual customer.

Supervision and Leadership in Tourism and Hospitality is for anyone whose goal is to become a supervisor or manager in this industry. Its aim is to help you develop a broad knowledge of the industry, as well as a sound understanding of the role of the supervisor and frontline manager in the industry.

Readers might think that supervision is something that comes before management. Well, in terms of organisational hierarchies, it does. However, a supervisor is the first line in management and the roles of the supervisor coincide with those of the manager. Of course, as you go up the organisational chart, the nature of the management role changes in focus to a more strategic direction. The frontline supervisor deals mainly with day-to-day issues. However, the issue of leadership is central to the roles of both supervisor and manager, and the two terms will be used interchangeably throughout this book. Many supervisors facing the challenges of day-to-day leadership argue that their role, although lacking the strategic, long-term focus of the manager, is the more complex of the two. On reading some of the case studies and thinking about the complex issues they present, you will probably agree!

In this book we will deal initially with the scope of the tourism and hospitality industry to give you an idea of the variety of opportunities that exist for supervisors and managers. This brief analysis of current trends will also assist newcomers to the industry with career planning. In the subsequent chapters we will cover, in general terms, the leadership role of the supervisor/frontline manager, and we will then look at the administrative aspects of this important job in more detail.

Working in this industry is both challenging and stimulating.

Frontline managers have an important role to play in maintaining the quality of service provided, sometimes during very busy and stressful periods. A sound understanding of workflow planning, staff scheduling and quality management (just a few of the topics covered in this book) will help to ensure that the operation you manage is a sustainable, profitable enterprise with satisfied customers and motivated staff.

CHAPTER ONE

the current
environment

LAST NIGHT THE COMPUTER SYSTEM WENT DOWN. WE ARE A LARGE home-delivery and takeaway operation with five operators taking orders over the phone and keying them into the computer. Normally these orders are relayed automatically to the different sections in the kitchen, but last night we had to run down the stairs with written orders. Orders for different sections of the kitchen (such as pizza or pasta) had to be prepared in duplicate or triplicate and handed to each chef. Then all orders had to be co-ordinated at the end. A few sheets of carbon paper would have helped! We probably lost a lot of business because some customers couldn't get through on the phone, delivery was slow and two orders disappeared in the chaos that occurred. Our takings for the night were definitely down and frustration levels were high both for staff and customers. The computer technician who came in the next day pointed out that a simple connection had come apart and that anyone with basic computer knowledge could have solved the problem.

The situation that developed in this home-delivery operation is not uncommon and illustrates the increasing role of technology in improving operational efficiency. This means that managers in all types of industries, including tourism and hospitality, need to develop their technical skills in order to deal with crises like the one above which inevitably occur. The leader's role in the tourism and hospitality industry, and the skills they require, will be discussed in detail in this and the following chapter.

The Australian Bureau of Statistics reports that the average

On completion of this chapter you will be able to:

- discuss the growth of the services sector, including tourism and hospitality
- describe the characteristics of service-based organisations
- identify the challenges facing supervisors in service-orientated environments
- describe current changes in the role of the supervisor in tourism and hospitality.

Australian household spends 27 per cent of its total food budget on meals out and takeaway food. In the highest income brackets this figure is as high as 35 per cent (ABS Cat. No. 6535.0, 1993–94). The operation mentioned on the previous page is an example of one of the many outlets that have developed in this country to service the current home-delivery trend. The situation that occurred in this company illustrates the importance of speedy and courteous service in the restaurant sector, as well as the increased reliance on computer technology.

In this chapter the growth of the tourism and hospitality sector, including job growth and demand for trained staff at supervisory and management levels, will be discussed. We will look closely at the characteristics of service organisations, for customer service is one of the most difficult challenges facing operators in this competitive environment. We will also cover the changing role of supervisors today.

Throughout this book the terms supervisor, manager and leader will be used interchangeably since supervisors are frontline managers. Supervisors face some of the biggest challenges since they are caught up in the day-to-day operation of their organisations, often being required to make quick decisions on a wide range of matters, more often than not during the busiest periods of the day.

Growth in the services sector

Tourism is one of the world's fastest growing industries. In Australia it is the country's largest foreign income-earner, growing from 1 million inbound tourists in 1984 to over 4 million in 1996, with an average annual increase of 13 per cent. Forecasts suggest that Australia can expect 7.6 million tourists to visit the country in 2007 (*Forecast*, June 1998).

However, tourism (domestic as well as international) is not the only source of business for the industry. Local residents, such as those calling the home-delivery service at the start of the chapter, are also contributing to increased demand in the hospitality sector. There are also numerous suppliers who can attribute their business success to the tourism and hospitality market. These include suppliers of fresh food, printers and publishers, advertising agencies and clothing manufacturers.

These few examples simply illustrate the extent to which the growth in tourism and hospitality contributes directly and indirectly

Fig. 1.1

Direct and indirect components of tourism.

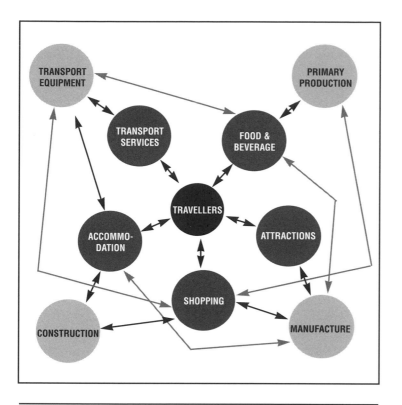

Source: *Forecast*, June 1997, Tourism Forecasting Council. Reproduced with permission.

to economic growth. Fig. 1.1 shows the relationship between some of these contributors.

Growth in employment

According to the report, *Tourism Workforce 2020*, employment in tourism occupations has grown by 3.7 per cent per annum over the past five years, three times the overall growth rate for jobs in Australia. The report also predicts that employment growth in the industry will continue at even higher rates (4 per cent per year) in the short term. In particular, the demand for supervisors in the restaurant and accommodation sectors is likely to increase steadily between 1995 and 2000. Certainly, anecdotal evidence from employers seems to indicate that there are shortages of supervisory level staff.

The above predictions are outlined in Table 1.1.

Table 1.1

Projected employment growth in designated tourism occupations, 1995–2000.

Source: Tourism Workforce 2020, Tourism Training Australia, 1996. © Australian National Training Authority.

Employment levels (000s)	1995 Total	2000 Total	Growth No.	Average Annual %
Restaurant and catering managing supervisors	26.3	28.3	2.0	1.4
Accommodation and tavern managing supervisors	29.4	32.7	3.3	2.2
Other tourism related occupations	373.0	459.7	86.7	4.6
Total	428.7	520.7	92.0	4.0

Characteristics of service-based organisations

A comparison between service operations and manufacturing operations is useful to show the differences between them. In the simplest terms, manufacturing is about things and service is about people (see Fig. 1.2).

Fig. 1.2

Difference between manufacturing and service operations.

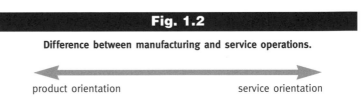

product orientation   service orientation

There are three main characteristics of service enterprises which can be used to highlight the differences between, say, a shoe manufacturer (which has a manufacturing orientation) and a travel agency (which has a service orientation).

Services are provided direct to the customer

In the manufacturing sector, products are generally developed and manufactured, and are then sent through a long distribution chain via wholesalers and retailers before they finally reach the customer. In the services sector, the service is provided direct to the customer and there is no opportunity to correct errors. If a waiter says the wrong thing, there is no taking it back!

Services are intangible

Services are abstract and cannot be described easily. 'Good' customer service, for example, is very hard to describe. Products, on the other hand, are tangible: they can be measured and checked according to a range of specifications. Cooked chips, for example, can be checked for freshness, size, temperature and saltiness.

Quality is defined by the customer's perceptions

While the quality of a product can be measured in terms of specifications, and customers are likely to reach a general agreement about the product's quality dimensions, services are based on complex and unique interactions between the service provider and the customer. The success or otherwise of this communication is largely determined by the customer's perception of the situation, with the result that there is far less agreement between customers about service since customers all have different needs and different ways of communicating.

When discussing tourism and hospitality operations, we find that there are products **and** services provided. For example, beds and linen are products, while room cleaning is a service. In a restaurant the meal is a product, enhanced by the service provided by the front of house staff. In different operations there is different emphasis on products and services. In five star hotels, for example, services are exceptionally important, while in a two star motel services would be very limited and you could be sure that nobody would carry your bag to your room. On the other hand, the main emphasis of a catering operation for an airline would be the manufacture of food products.

One of the distinctive features of the hospitality industry is the fact that many of the products are perishable. This adds to the complexity of the situation since waste leads to reduced profits and stale ingredients lead to unhappy customers. Thus, in comparison with the manufacturing operation, which mostly produces non-perishable items, the hospitality operation must face the problems inherent in being a service provider **plus** the challenges that inevitably arise from dealing with perishable inputs and outputs.

The final and important comparison that must be made is that many products of the tourism and hospitality industry cannot be sold at a later date. In tourism and hospitality, certain products (airline tickets and hotel beds, for example) cannot be held over and discounted. If an airline seat or hotel bed is empty, that revenue is lost. In a fashion store, on the other hand, clothes can be discounted and sold at a later date.

Challenges in service-orientated environments

The following challenges have always faced supervisors working in tourism and hospitality organisations.

Complexity of the situation

Because supervisors are working with people, both other staff and customers, communication is complex and high levels of training and judgement are required in order to make effective decisions. Customers are very demanding. A customer might ask for information on trout fishing at Lake Tekapo in New Zealand or a client might ask for an item not listed on the menu. This is quite unlike, say, a hardware store where, for example, the salesperson would not be asked, or be able to, modify products to suit the customer's needs.

Immediate response to customers' needs

In the hospitality industry, where guests' physical needs are being catered for, the challenges are greater because customers want their needs satisfied immediately. The tired or hungry guest has very little patience. In many other retail outlets, the customer is generally happy to wait until the product they want is ordered in or located elsewhere.

Avoiding lost opportunities

This issue has been mentioned already. In industry jargon it means making sure there are 'heads on beds' and 'bums on seats'. Lost opportunities to make money are just that — lost opportunities.

Minimising waste

Where a business opportunity is lost, there is often a cost incurred for waste. This could be for staffing costs because staff were idle and/or for perishable products which could not be utilised. In the scenario at the start of the chapter, staff were not being used effectively and no doubt waste would have occurred as a result of reduced business.

Organising working hours

The 24-hour nature of many hospitality operations and the seven-days-a-week operation of most tourism attractions has important implications for the supervisor. Rostering, staffing and training require careful attention as stress levels can be high when staff move from one shift cycle to another or forego opportunities to be with family and friends.

Dealing with part-time and casual workers

The industry is characterised by a labour force which is predominantly part-time and casual. This has important implications for training and the provision of quality service.

Controlling costs of labour and labour turnover

Being labour intensive, tourism and hospitality operations are under constant pressure to constrain labour costs. Taken too far, this strategy leaves the operation understaffed during busy periods and gives rise to a number of other short-term and long-term problems, such as low morale and poor service.

Recent changes in the role of the supervisor

During the last decade or so, organisational changes in the workplace have resulted in a more complex role for the supervisor employed in the tourism and hospitality industry, as outlined below.

Greater responsibility

Trends towards flatter organisations have led to increased levels of responsibility for supervisors, who now make many decisions previously referred to management.

Diverse customer expectations

The industry now has an extensive customer base, which is far from homogeneous. Supervisors and staff need to meet the needs of a broad range of customers in terms of age, income, interests, cultural background, level of education and many other factors.

Heightened employee expectations

Where there is an emphasis on teamwork the supervisor needs to develop strategies to improve communication. Worker participation levels are high in the modern workplace and workers expect to be consulted about changes to workplace practices. Increased participation in training and education by tourism and hospitality students means that supervisors are dealing both with well-trained and educated entry level staff (with high career expectations) and with staff whose skills are very limited. These relatively unskilled employees are often in the industry for reasons other than career development. This means that supervisors often have a mix of skilled and unskilled employees with very different career aspirations.

Developing multicultural customer base and workforce

The tourism and hospitality industry is characterised by a multi-cultural customer base, and the languages and cultural knowledge of employees need to be utilised effectively. Both customers and employees often have English as a second language and this needs to be taken into account from a communications point of view.

Changing jobs

Multiskilling means that staff are now able to perform a range of tasks. As specialisation and routine work continues to diminish, training is increasingly required to develop a multiskilled workforce. Such employees are valuable because they are flexible and generally more responsive to customer needs.

Changing workforce

One of the most recent changes to the workforce has been the entry of a significant number of women, especially in the older age groups. There is also a trend towards shorter working hours, with many employees favouring part-time and casual employment. Youth unemployment is still high and this resource is readily available for entry level positions.

Changing employee education

Young people are now staying at school longer which means that the entry level employee is both older and better educated.

All of these factors illustrate that today's supervisor is working in an environment in which there has been a number of significant developments, and these have added considerably to the challenges that have always been part of this job.

Discussion questions

1 *Is a supervisor a manager?*
2 *Are all customers who visit hospitality establishments tourists?*
3 *Give one indicator of growth in tourism and one in hospitality.*
4 *What are the characteristics of service organisations? Explain, using examples.*
5 *List and describe five challenges facing the supervisor in the tourism and hospitality industry.*

Case study

Charlene had completed her cookery apprenticeship and had worked at two different establishments by the time she started working at the Mansfield Park Hotel. When she had been there for five months she was promoted to Chef de Partie which meant that she was in charge of the work of three apprentices and a kitchen hand. She found it very difficult to give instructions to her staff who had previously been working alongside her in the team. Language differences had not presented a problem when they had been working (and socialising) together, but they were now making it more difficult for her to give instructions and to delegate tasks. In particular, the kitchen hand did not like taking instructions from a woman and would always go to one of the apprentices if he had a problem. The apprentices all had different levels of experience and different skills.

Charlene has come to you for advice since she is struggling with

SUMMARY

Steady growth in tourism and hospitality is predicted to continue into the next decade, and this will undoubtedly lead to an increased demand for supervisors across a range of sectors of the industry. Organisations involved in the industry have a strong focus on quality service and the customer. For the frontline manager, this offers a number of challenges, and these challenges are continually increasing with the important developments which are occurring in its customer base and in the organisational structure and level of education of its workforce. These factors are placing high demands on the skills and knowledge of today's supervisor.

her supervisory role and finding it more difficult than she had realised it would be.

Explain the basic differences between a frontline employee and a supervisor to Charlene.

Look at the challenges facing supervisors and relate each of these to a situation such as this one, giving Charlene some ideas about why her new role is proving more difficult than she thought it would be. (There is no need at this stage to tell her how to meet these challenges; that can wait for later chapters.)

In addition, explain to Charlene how the role of a supervisor has changed in recent times.

CHAPTER TWO

the role of the
supervisor

For me, the management of teaspoons is the first thing I look at in every new job. I even ask the question in the interview — how often do you run out of teaspoons? They probably think I'm mad. However, in every place I've worked, teaspoon stock management indicates whether managers and supervisors know what they are doing. In some places, stocks are so low that staff hide the teaspoons or steal them from other staff and other departments. So much for teamwork! What does all of this tell you about the place? The meaning of words like 'planning', 'organising' and 'monitoring' becomes apparent when looked at in the context of the teaspoon situation. If convention centres, hotels or restaurants can't manage teaspoon stocks, how can they manage their finances? One fellow I know worked on a cruise ship where the teaspoons were silver plated. The staff mutinied because they were treated badly and threw most of the teaspoons overboard through the wire mesh on the portholes. The waiters tied the few remaining teaspoons around their waists and had to stir for each customer. I assure you, teaspoons tell you everything you need to know about the management of a place.

On completion of this chapter you will be able to:
- describe the leadership role of the supervisor
- outline the skills required for effective supervision
- explain the functions of a manager or supervisor
- give examples of legal and ethical issues which face supervisors.

The above discussion about teaspoons and their role as indicators of successful management, or otherwise, highlights one of the important roles of the supervisor: ensuring that sufficient resources are available. This involves planning and organising, as well as checking, in this case on the availability of teaspoons, before good service can be provided. However, the story also illustrates another vital aspect of supervision: the ability to lead and manage people. Without the support of people, supervisors cannot achieve the goals set for them. In the above instance, the lack of support for the supervisor was even more obvious when staff threw the teaspoons overboard. Supervisors need the support of staff and cannot afford to have them sabotage operations.

The leadership role of the supervisor

The primary role of the supervisor is to ensure that a group of people work together to achieve the goals set by the business. With a tourist information centre, for example, this means ensuring that physical resources (such as brochures) are available, correct and up to date. Since service is so important, staff training is one of the supervisor's most critical roles. Managing physical and human resources to achieve customer service goals requires planning, organising, staffing, directing and controlling. Each of these terms will be described in detail in this chapter. The frontline manager or supervisor plays a key role in the interface between frontline staff and more senior management. For this reason, effective communication flow is essential — in both directions. Here the supervisor plays a pivotal role.

Functions of the supervisor

Anyone in a leadership position performs the five functions illustrated in Fig. 2.1 and expanded on below.

Fig. 2.1

Five functions of a manager.

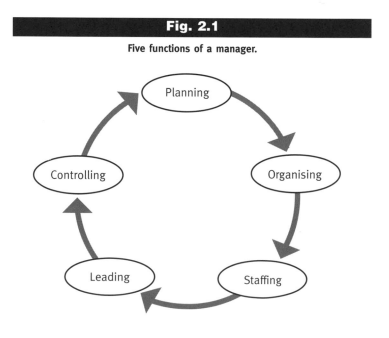

Planning

In order to achieve the goals of your work team, you need to plan a pathway and decide what is needed and how things should be done. Lack of planning will inevitably lead to chaos. In restaurants, the term mis-en-place means preparing for service. If all the tables have been set and the crockery and cutlery stocks have been cleaned and polished, if the garnishes have been prepared and other requirements have been set out carefully on the sideboard, then the staff will find that service will flow smoothly. This is an example of short-term planning. But supervisors also need to plan long-term by looking, for example, at staff requirements for that long weekend several weeks away to make sure that enough trained staff will be on duty. Rostering is just one aspect of long-term planning for the supervisor in a restaurant and they would need to take into account such things as the level of business anticipated, staff requests and labour costs.

Staffing

A supervisor needs to make sure that there are enough trained staff on duty to provide adequate (or superior) levels of service. Sometimes this involves advertising for staff, interviewing them and selecting the most suitable candidates. The supervisor must also ensure that these people are trained and motivated to achieve team goals.

Organising

As a supervisor, you need to allocate duties to individuals. Organisation means ensuring that every task is performed effectively and efficiently. This can involve delegating tasks to people who do not generally do them and taking on some of them yourself. By organising duties in this way, situations in which everyone turns around and says, 'I thought you were going to do it!' will be avoided. Organising also involves allocating physical resources. In the case of the teaspoon shortage, you would have to ration them carefully since planning procedures had clearly failed.

Directing

This involves giving instructions, or telling and showing people what to do. Supervisors are very important role models and staff will copy their behaviour. Your dealings with customers, in particular, will be closely watched by staff and imitated by them. The way in which instructions are given is important and this will be one of the topics of discussion in the following chapters on motivation and leadership. In the current environment staff expect a coaching style of directing, whereas in earlier times bosses were far more autocratic.

Controlling

Supervisors need to check that things are on track. If physical resources are constantly running low, then regular orders need to be updated. If staff are not performing to the required standard, the reasons for this need to be investigated and resolved.

As you can see, a supervisor needs to carefully balance these functions. Too much time spent on planning and too little on checking means that the supervisor will never know if the plans are working. Too little time spent on planning will lead to chaos in the directing phase. Checks conducted in the controlling phase can produce ideas for improving planning, staffing and organising.

Skills for effective supervision

Robert L. Katz (1974) has suggested that there are three types of skills required for effective management: technical, people and conceptual.

Technical skills

These are the skills required to get the job done. Since training is such an important part of the supervisor's role, it is essential that the supervisor be a skilled technician in all the areas they are managing. For example, it might be necessary for them to have skills in cooking, taking computer reservations, providing information, attending rooms, supervising children, providing nutritional advice and monitoring chemical levels in the hot tub. Supervisors who do not have the necessary technical skills find it hard to retain their credibility with staff. They need these skills for situations in which they have to assist others in the team and particularly for trouble-shooting when there is a technical problem.

People skills

In leading a team, a supervisor needs to be sensitive to the needs of others, to communicate effectively and to bring the group together so that they can achieve mutually agreed goals. Listening, questioning, communicating clearly, handling conflicts, and providing support and praise are all people skills.

Conceptual skills

A supervisor does a lot of thinking, especially when planning or analysing why things aren't going as expected. Decision-making and problem-solving are conceptual skills. For the supervisor, conceptual skills are necessary for reasonably short-term planning. Senior managers, on the other hand, require conceptual skills for long-term, strategic planning as they need to look at issues such as marketing several years ahead.

In comparing frontline managers (supervisors) and senior managers, senior managers would need fewer up-to-date technical skills (for example, they wouldn't need to know how modern cellar equipment works) but they would need very good conceptual skills for such aspects of the job as long-term financial planning. Thus at different levels and in different occupations the mix of skills might be different. This is illustrated in Fig. 2.2.

Fig. 2.2

Different mix of skills required by frontline managers and senior managers.

conceptual skills	conceptual skills
people skills	
	people skills
technical skills	
	technical skills

Using a similar model to Katz's, Henry Mintzberg (1973) has suggested that the supervisor has three broad roles: interpersonal (people skills), informational (people and technical skills) and decision-making (conceptual).

Legal issues facing supervisors

A number of legal requirements have to be upheld by supervisors on behalf of their employers. For example, a bar supervisor must ensure that alcohol is served in the correct measure and that there is no substitution of inferior products.

The following legislation has implications for supervisors working in tourism and hospitality.

Trade Practices

This legislation is about providing the goods and services advertised. This is particularly relevant to the travel sector.

Industrial Relations

Meeting award and other contractual guidelines for pay and other conditions of work is part of the supervisor's role. Limiting the length of shifts and providing breaks are examples. Employers should also adhere to statute laws relating to industrial relations, such as Equal Employment Opportunity and Unfair Dismissal legislation.

Occupational Health and Safety

Occupational Health and Safety legislation requires employers to provide a safe place of work and safe systems of work. The supervisor's role is to ensure that safe systems of work are developed and enforced. Tools and equipment need to be checked for safety; keyboard operators must be provided with regular breaks and ergonomic furniture owing to the repetitive nature of their work.

Workers' Compensation

Employees who are injured during their employment are entitled to workers' compensation. The supervisor's role is to minimise work-

place accidents, primarily through preventative measures such as safety training, and to assist in the rehabilitation of workers when they return to work.

Liquor

Liquor legislation covers the sale of alcohol on licensed premises and outlines limitations such as hours and venues. Serving minors is illegal under this legislation. Responsible service of alcohol is an important issue for supervisors who need to provide their staff with training and support on this topic.

Food

Food acts require that food be prepared and handled in a hygienic way in order to prevent food poisoning. Staff training and the development of systems and procedures for safe food handling are proactive measures that should be implemented by supervisors working in the hospitality industry.

Insurance

Some insurances, particularly in the travel industry, are compulsory. One of the roles of the supervisor is to put in place procedures to keep the number of claims to a minimum which in turn results in reduced premiums.

Taxation

Employers are obliged to declare accurate business income and to deduct taxes from the wages and salaries of employees. Employees should not be paid in cash, without deducting tax, and tills should balance at the end of the trading period.

Anti-discrimination

Staff and customers cannot be subjected to discrimination on the basis of such factors as sex or physical impairment. This is an important consideration for supervisors when selecting or promoting employees.

Ethical issues facing supervisors

Favouritism is one of the most common complaints about supervisors. Being consistent in handling staff is essential in order to avoid perceived inequity. Such inequity can arise from the amount of training or performance counselling given, from promotion of certain employees and from shifts allocated when rostering. Staff often see it as unfair if only some people are involved in conversations, or if only some are given information or attention. Ethical treatment of staff is fair treatment of staff and one of the surest ways for a supervisor to gain support and respect.

Another area, which is partly under the control of the supervisor, is allocation of staff. Where there are inadequate numbers of employees, everyone is placed under stress, especially if the supervisor promotes overbooking as a hedge against cancellations. Large numbers of casual and relatively untrained staff also add to stress levels at work. The issue of appropriate numbers of adequately trained staff is the most common dilemma for the supervisor — if too many employees are allocated, management will certainly be unhappy about the labour cost!

Confidentiality is an important issue for the supervisor, made particularly complex when hotel staff suspect a guest might be acting illegally, such as being involved in drug dealing. An interesting issue concerning customer confidentiality appeared in the news recently. A resort had reportedly kept records of a guest's activities which were later raised in a divorce case. The resort's efforts to assemble marketing and other information about their guest had clearly gone beyond the bounds of personal privacy.

In the daily operation of tourism and hospitality establishments, supervisors are confronted with many legislative and ethical issues. A good knowledge of relevant legislation, and support in terms of policies, is invaluable in this regard. Supervisors in workplaces where such policies do not exist should discuss this issue with their superiors. Employer associations, such as the National Restaurant and Catering Association, the Australian Hotels Association or the International Association of Travel Agents (IATA), can provide invaluable legal advice to members.

Discussion questions

1 *If you were supervising in a kitchen you would be managing both physical and human resources. Describe how you would manage these resources and decide which of the two would be more important in achieving the objectives of the kitchen brigade.*

2 *Explain, using industry examples, how lack of planning can lead to problems later on.*

3 *If you were a supervisor in a travel agency, what form of controlling, or checking, would be necessary?*

4 *Compare the job of an accountant with that of a public relations manager in terms of the skills described by Katz.*

5 *List in order the most common ethical issues facing supervisors in tourism and hospitality.*

SUMMARY

In this chapter we have dealt with the five functions of all managers, including the frontline manager: planning, staffing, organising, directing and controlling. These functions are all linked. Directing staff is one of the topics of the following chapters on motivation and leadership and Chapter 8 on delegation and control. We have also looked at the skills required for effective supervision and have adopted Katz's categorisation of these skills as technical, people and conceptual. The weighting of these skills would of course differ with seniority, the nature of the organisation (service or manufacturing) and the type of work involved. Legal and ethical issues relevant to the supervisor have also been discussed.

Case study

Liam was applying for a promotion to a supervisor's position and needed to decide how he would sell himself at the interview. His family suggested that he promote himself as a 'people person' since he was working in a service industry. They suggested that he talk about communication in teams, about meetings, conflict management and teamwork. Liam knew that he was good with people, having coached a football team, and thought that he should stress listening and questioning skills, and verbal and non-verbal communication as well.

Refer to the three skill types of an effective manager suggested by Katz and tell this applicant whether you think he will get the job and why. Make suggestions for improving his interview performance in terms of the skills he has to offer and explain these to him.

CHAPTER THREE

motivation

ONE OF MY FIRST EXPERIENCES AS A SUPERVISOR TAUGHT ME A LOT. When I started working at the motel complex I suggested that we start an Employee of the Month system. Everyone was very enthusiastic about my new idea to motivate staff. We also planned to put the person's name in the local newspaper. When the employee was chosen for the first award, she was very excited. Soon afterwards, however, things began to happen. First, she was not happy to have her picture in the paper because she thought her friends would think it was silly. Secondly, some of the staff started to question why she had been chosen. Before I arrived the staff had worked together really well, but this initiative caused so much dissention that two factions emerged. This taught me to think through plans better and to reach agreement with my work team about changes that might affect them. I thought that this award would have been a simple solution to improving morale and increasing motivation. I had to learn that people are more complex than I had realised and that being a supervisor was going to be quite a challenge. One staff member even suggested that Employee of the Month was not consistent with EEO principles. I immediately realised that it was time to develop my knowledge of Equal Employment Opportunity legislation and motivational theories.

The new manager thought that the scheme she introduced would be a sure success and was surprised at the way it turned out. Employee of the Month schemes are widely used to motivate staff and are generally very successful. One example of outstanding success was the scheme introduced at a Mercure Hotel in Sydney where the Employee of the Month was offered the incentive of pushing the General Manager out of a plane — wearing a parachute, of course. Guests were given questionnaires about service and the staff member scoring the highest points was selected as Employee of the Month. In this case, two employees were victorious and the strategy proved a resounding success.

Any discussion about motivation needs to take individual differences and perceptions into account. Different staff members will be motivated by different things. In this chapter we will look at four theories of motivation and you will have the opportunity to develop your own motivational theory at the end of the chapter. For proficient management, it is a must for supervisors and managers to develop a personal philosophy as a basis for the management of their staff.

What is motivation?

Motivation is the thing that induces people to act. Leaders need to persuade people to act in certain ways. In a workplace situation, staff must first be motivated to follow procedures. This can be done in a positive way by offering rewards, or in a negative way by threatening staff who do not comply with requirements. Both methods can be effective, and both can be used by the same leader. It has been said of Australia that 'there are too many carrots and not enough sticks'. This means that there are few ways in which employees can be forced to do things, other than by dismissal. And of course dismissal is not really threatening if there are other jobs or other opportunities. These other jobs and opportunities are the carrots. If a person is constantly faced with a range of rewarding scenarios, it is difficult to select one which will be a powerful motivator. Staff may, for example, become indifferent to Employee of the Month schemes. However the hotel manager at the Mercure was very clever in that he introduced novelty and fun into the reward system.

In many other countries the threat of dismissal is taken far more seriously. Rewards are also perceived differently. This reinforces the point made earlier on the importance of understanding people's perceptions as to whether making an effort to achieve a goal will be worth the reward. To make life even more complicated, sometimes people are rewarded for the wrong behaviour. A staff member who regularly arrives late to find that other people have done the setting

up is rewarded for this behaviour. Likewise, someone who is paid the same as everyone else but finds ways to avoid working hard is rewarded for laziness.

Looking at what motivates people, and how to lead them, is essential for every manager. There are a number of theories that can be used to stimulate ideas and four of them will be presented later in this chapter. Firstly, however, let's look at some of the symptoms of poor motivation and compare them with some of the indicators of high motivation.

Symptoms of poor morale and lack of motivation

There are many symptoms of poor motivation, but in general terms they reveal themselves as a lack of interest in getting the job done correctly and getting it done quickly. Although they may be indicators of poor motivation, the lack of efficiency and effectiveness could also be the result of tiredness, personal problems, poor work design, repetitive work, lack of discipline, interpersonal conflict, lack of training, and so on. Some of these can be linked to motivation but others, such as repetitive work, have nothing to do with motivation. A person may be highly motivated but find the work physically impossible. For the moment, however, we will focus on motivation, while making the assumption that when such symptoms occur the reasons for them will be fully investigated.

In Table 3.1 a scale is used to measure behaviour which may indicate poor motivation.

Table 3.1

Indicators of morale and job satisfaction.

Tick appropriate box in each instance.

Adherence to standard procedures

excellent	good	average	below average	poor
☐	☐	☐	☐	☐

Care for safety, self and others

excellent	good	average	below average	poor
☐	☐	☐	☐	☐

Initiative in finding tasks needed to be done

excellent	good	average	below average	poor
☐	☐	☐	☐	☐

Looking for areas in which other people need help

excellent	good	average	below average	poor
☐	☐	☐	☐	☐

Being co-operative and willing

excellent	good	average	below average	poor
☐	☐	☐	☐	☐

Interacting positively with customers

excellent	good	average	below average	poor
☐	☐	☐	☐	☐

Responding to requests immediately

excellent	good	average	below average	poor
☐	☐	☐	☐	☐

Working quickly

excellent	good	average	below average	poor
☐	☐	☐	☐	☐

Contributing ideas

excellent	good	average	below average	poor
☐	☐	☐	☐	☐

As you can see from the scale, a poor score on 'working quickly' could be related to motivation, however a leader needs to be aware that factors such as shortages (of equipment or supplies) could contribute to inefficiency.

Theories of motivation

Four theories of motivation are presented in this chapter and these can be used in conjunction with your own experience in the workplace to test your ideas on the subject.

Numerous books have been written on the topic of motivation which you are encouraged to read. Experienced managers are also a valuable source of ideas on this subject.

The aim of this chapter is for you to develop your own framework or theory of motivation. While it is unlikely that your 'model' will remain unchanged over time, it will be a useful starting point. During your working life as a manager you will have many opportunities to test and modify your conceptual framework. This is known as 'action learning'.

The first of the theories covered here is Maslow's. While it has been argued that this model is too simplistic and suffers from a lack of hard evidence, it continues to be popularly adopted. The second theory, developed by Frederick Herzberg, looks at motivation and demotivation, while the final two theories focus on perceptions of effort and reward and on the links between behaviour and reward.

Maslow's hierarchy of needs

Maslow's hierarchy of needs is a simple concept which has had universal appeal despite its many criticisms, and his model has endured since first proposed in 1954. In Maslow's hierarchy there are five levels of needs (Fig. 3.1), and these are discussed below, with examples from the tourism and hospitality workplace. Maslow argues that as needs are satisfied at one level the next level becomes dominant.

Physical

Physical needs are mainly food and rest. In the hospitality industry, shiftwork can play havoc with one's sleep patterns, particularly if shifts are allocated randomly without allowing enough rest in between, and this can result in poor motivation. Working in hot kitchens, standing on one's feet all day and not getting enough breaks, are other physical reasons why staff become poorly motivated. Their physical needs are not being met.

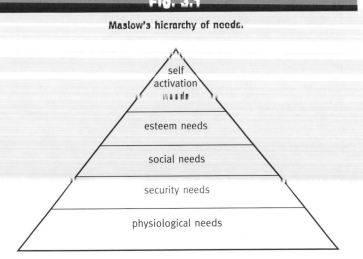

Fig. 3.1

Maslow's hierarchy of needs.

- self activation needs
- esteem needs
- social needs
- security needs
- physiological needs

Security

Feeling secure is a very important need for most people. We need to know where our next pay cheque is coming from and that we can provide for ourselves and our families. In some parts of the industry, there are very high numbers of casual staff who never know how much work they can expect. It suits management to have flexible labour, but seldom suits staff to have flexible pay packets and no job security. Other needs involved here include working in a safe environment in which there are no physical or other risks: cuts, falls and burns are not uncommon in the hospitality industry and repetitive strain injury is a threat in the travel industry where so much time is spent at the keyboard.

Social

People's social needs involve feelings of belonging. This is achieved when the work team is cohesive and co-operative. Social harmony is a special challenge for supervisors in tourism and hospitality because staff change constantly due to labour turnover or different work allocations and shifts. Airline crews on international flights generally work with a new team on each assignment and may not meet those individuals again for months or even years. In the ideal workplace, stable teams are able to develop over a period of time. For cohesive teams to develop, success in achieving positive group goals is vital. If this level of cohesion does not develop, job design factors need to be given greater attention and each team member's role needs to be clearly defined. If such strategies are put in place, service will begin to flow smoothly as a consequence.

Esteem

Self-esteem is the way people feel about themselves. Winning prizes or awards, being praised or having one's ideas implemented all help to develop self-esteem. Esteem needs are met when employees are allowed to work autonomously and when their efforts are recognised. Promotion and higher status meet esteem needs.

Self-actualisation

Self-actualisation generally occurs when a person feels they are achieving their personal goals. Training and career progression both help staff to feel that they are reaching their personal potential. To meet the individual employee's need for self-actualisation, jobs need to be interesting and challenging.

Maslow's theory is a useful tool for looking at people's needs. At different times an individual may experience different needs, and different people often have different needs. One employee might be prepared to work hard for low pay because he is being trained and because he is on a career path that will lead somewhere he desires in the longer term. This promotion would allow him to meet his esteem and self-actualisation needs. Another employee may be paying off a loan and, for her, security is more important. If she is given a job in which she feels secure, she may be highly motivated. Yet another employee might be demotivated because her job keeps her away from family and friends, and these social needs are important to her and cannot be fulfilled in the workplace. On the other hand, there are many employees in this industry who are highly motivated by the social nature of their work.

Herzberg's two-factor theory

Another theorist, Frederick Herzberg (1959) proposed that there are two types of factors: one lot of factors motivate and cause satisfaction; the other (which he called 'hygiene factors') may cause dissatisfaction. Herzberg suggested that only the esteem and self-actualisation needs suggested by Maslow motivate people to work harder. If a person's effort is acknowledged, their self-esteem increases and they will be encouraged to make an even greater effort.

The hygiene factors are such aspects of the job as a safe physical environment, job security and the social environment that most people take for granted. On their own they would not motivate anyone to work harder. One wouldn't hear someone say, 'I've got air-conditioning in the office, I feel really motivated to work for this employer'. Nor would someone say, 'I work in a safe workplace, I feel really motivated'. Herzberg suggests, however, that if there are problems with the physical or social environment, or with safety and security, this could cause workers to become demotivated.

Vroom's expectancy theory

Victor Vroom's theory (1964) is quite sophisticated but at its core is the concept of 'expectancy'. Vroom argues that a worker will become motivated if, firstly, he or she expects to be able to achieve the goal set by management. This is stage one, as illustrated in Fig. 3.2. If a person does not have the skills or training, or if there are other hurdles, their perception will be that the goal is unachievable. Therefore they do not expect to achieve the goal and are not motivated to try.

Fig. 3.2

Expectancy theory.

$$\text{Motivation} = \left(\text{effort} \xrightarrow{\text{will lead to}} \text{performance}\right)\left(\text{performance} \xrightarrow{\text{will lead to}} \text{attractive outcomes}\right)$$

STAGE **1**   STAGE **2**

In the second stage, the person expects to achieve an outcome. Sometimes these outcomes are promised but not delivered. For example, in the tourism and hospitality industry, promises are often made and broken about having Sundays off. Likewise expectations about pay rises may not be realised. In stage two, therefore, the employee is asking, 'Do I trust you to deliver the outcome if I achieve the goals you set?'. So, while stage one is about effort, stage two is about trust. Expectations about effort leading to achievement of performance goals, and the achievement of performance goals leading to positive outcomes, are the two stages illustrated in Fig. 3.2.

Finally, Vroom looks at the value that employees place on outcomes or rewards. In the earlier discussion about Employee of the Month, an employee would first have to believe that achievement of the award were possible and, secondly, they would have to view the outcome as something they would find personally rewarding. If a person does not expect to achieve the stated goal and does not expect to value the outcome, then they will not be motivated to try.

Vroom's theory is thus about people as individuals. All have different perceptions of a situation, and different expectations, which will affect the ways in which they can be motivated.

Behaviourist theories

Another group of theorists look, instead, at people's responsive behaviour. These responses lead to positive and negative outcomes, which in turn influence future behaviour. These theorists are more concerned with behaviour than with perception. In brief, they argue that behaviour is influenced by one or more of the four following outcomes.

Positive reinforcement

If something positive happens, a person will be rewarded and the behaviour will increase. When this happens more than once, the behaviour will become increasingly entrenched and the person will be motivated to continue even in the absence of reward. An example of this is good telephone selling techniques developed during training and reinforced over time.

Another example of the application of positive reinforcement in the workplace is an organisation where effort is recognised and rewarded. In such an environment staff are motivated and productive. This has a flow-on effect for customer service because the environment is positive. In addition, employees will continue to exert this level of effort in the absence of a supervisor because behaviours resulting from positive reinforcement are firmly established and resistant to change. Finally, the reinforcement of one behaviour (through praise or recognition) will have an effect on other behaviours leading, for example, to reduced absenteeism.

There are numerous ways in which positive reinforcement can be given, including attention, praise, choice of shifts, late starts, early finishes, bonuses, prizes and awards, and training and promotion.

Punishment

If something negative happens (such as criticism), the behaviour will diminish (particularly if the person punishing or criticising is present). The person will become demotivated and this will have a flow-on effect to other behaviours.

Extinction

If no outcome follows a behaviour, the behaviour is unlikely to be repeated. This is the case if effort goes unnoticed.

Negative reinforcement

This is a more difficult concept. Here, behaviour that prevents a negative outcome increases. This is known as avoidance behaviour. If you find that using a towel to pick up hot items avoids burns, you will use the towel all the time as an avoidance behaviour. In this case the burn is a negative consequence which has been avoided. This will cause the behaviour of using a towel to increase (because it works!).

These ideas are summarised in Fig. 3.3.

Fig. 3.3

Theory of consequences.

	Positive consequence	Negative consequence
Applied	Positive reinforcement	Punishment/criticism
Withheld	Extinction	Negative reinforcement

To apply this theory you would need to look very carefully at a range of consequences. If, for example, a room attendant found that she could sleep on one of the hotel beds for an hour and still get the job done, then this behaviour would be positively reinforced. The threat of being caught and fired (punishment) may not be seen as serious enough to counteract the positive outcome. If, on the other hand, a supervisor was constantly popping in to see what the room attendants were doing, the staff might increase their level of work (or at least look busy) to avoid a negative consequence. This would be a negative reinforcement. However, if the room attendants were paid according to the number of rooms cleaned (properly), this would be positive reinforcement for hard work.

Your personal theory of motivation

As someone in charge of others, you need to have a plan for how you will approach the challenging issue of motivation. In the mind map

Fig. 3.4

Mind map – a personal theory of motivation.

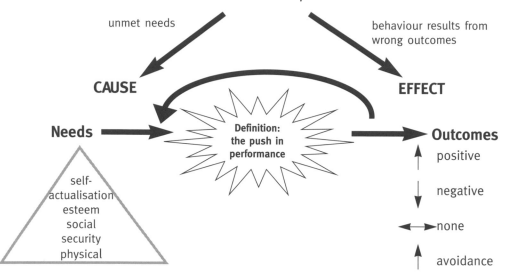

Is it a motivation problem?

unmet needs

behaviour results from wrong outcomes

CAUSE

EFFECT

Needs

Definition: the push in performance

Outcomes

↑ positive

↓ negative

←→ none

↑ avoidance

self-actualisation
esteem
social
security
physical

MOTIVATION

training
support
work design
hurdles

praise
prizes
incentives
'freebees'
external training

1
Each employee has different needs and expectations.

2
Understand performance and capability (skills, knowledge attitudes).

3
Find **valued achievable** goals **linked** to positive consequences.

Reward groups and individuals

---

illustrated in Fig. 3.4, a supervisor has developed her own ideas about the topic. As her experience as a supervisor and manager grows, she may have to revise her views. However, this is a good starting point for a personal action theory of motivation which can over time be tested and refined.

Discussion questions

1 *Normally full-time staff are paid the same amount on a regular basis. Do you think that this is soon taken for granted (as Herzberg's theory of hygiene factors suggests)? Discuss.*
2 *How can pay become an effective motivator?*
3 *What assumptions would you make about the motivation of a female worker of non-English-speaking background with two young children?*
4 *Explain in detail how you would check these assumptions and motivate this person.*
5 *Describe your personal motivation theory and illustrate it with a diagram.*
6 *Apply and evaluate your personal motivation theory.*

Case study

Vito was one of the most successful managers I had ever watched in action. I asked him how he managed to motivate his staff so well. He said that his approach was simple: specific steps and clear results. He always knew exactly what he wanted his staff to do and what the results were to be. All he had to do was communicate this clearly to them. However, the number of staff resigning from his department was higher than in any other department.

Explain why you think some of the staff in his department were motivated to stay and work hard, while others were motivated to leave.

SUMMARY

In this chapter we have briefly outlined four theories of motivation. Maslow has divided our needs into five categories and argues that people are motivated to meet their needs at one of the five levels in the hierarchy. As one level of need is satisfied, the individual is motivated to achieve satisfaction at the next level. Herzberg argues that of Maslow's categories only esteem and self-actualisation motivate, while the others are taken for granted, having an impact on the individual and causing dissatisfaction only if they are absent. Vroom's theory introduces the concept of expectancy: if a person expects to succeed, he or she will be motivated to put in the effort and reap the rewards. The behaviourists also focus on outcomes, proposing that behaviour is influenced by the consequences that follow. Quite simply, praise or other positive outcomes following behaviour will cause it to increase.

CHAPTER FOUR

leadership

I HAD GONE HOME BY THEN. PAUL WAS ON DUTY. A COUPLE OF GUYS got a bit restless and started a fight. Paul pressed the panic button right away and called the cops. Some young police came in swinging their batons and all hell broke loose. The guys turned on them. The place emptied in no time. What's the cure for panic? Experience. You have to know how to deal with guys like these quietly. Usually one of their mates will take them home if you ask nicely. That way nobody loses face. If you panic in a situation like this, it escalates. An experienced manager knows how to act in different situations. Sure, I sometimes have to call the cops, but not at the first sign of trouble. You have to be able to read situations before you act. Like everyone, Paul will have to learn the hard way.

Leadership is quite a controversial subject and everyone you talk to will probably have different ideas on what it is that constitutes a good leader. According to the manager in the above scenario a leader is someone who is experienced enough to know when to panic and when not to panic. He attributes his leadership ability to his experience. Others argue that leaders are born, not made.

In this chapter we will look at two broad schools of leadership thinking, the 'best way' school and the 'situational' school. The first group says that good leadership can be reasonably well defined and that this style will be consistent in most situations. Theorists from the second group say that a person's leadership style has to change according to different situations and that flexibility is the key. In developing your own philosophy of leadership you will need to decide how much flexibility you wish to build into your model.

What is leadership?

Leadership is about harnessing people's energy towards achieving organisational goals. According to Stoner, Collins and Yetton (1985), 'leadership is the process of directing and influencing the task related activities of group members'.

Theories of leadership

'One Best Way' theories

These theories aim to describe the traits and behaviours that make managers effective.

Trait theories

Researchers looking at the way the best leaders led looked first at their personality traits. They tried to analyse traits such as extroversion, intelligence, confidence, initiative, and so on to see whether they could develop a consistent list of traits for leaders. What they found, however, was that different leaders had different traits. If you were to compare Australia's last three Prime Ministers, you would agree that these leaders could not be defined in terms of the same traits.

Style theories

More recent studies have looked at leadership styles. Researchers at Ohio State University studied employee-orientated behaviour and task-orientated behaviour, and these concepts were used by Blake and Mouton (1966) as the basis for their managerial grid. This is illustrated in Fig. 4.1 in which concern for people and concern for production form each axis. Where a manager is low in both concern for people and concern for production, he or she is described as 'impoverished'. If a manager shows high concern for people and low concern for production, this is known as 'country club management'. It would be interesting to find out from club managers whether this correctly describes their leadership styles. It implies that they have little concern for getting the job done, but work well with people and are concerned about their welfare. Where a manager is task but not people orientated, this is described as 'authoritarian'. In the case study at the end of the chapter you will meet a housekeeper who insists that her authoritarian style is the best approach to running her busy department. Finally, Blake and Mouton describe the high

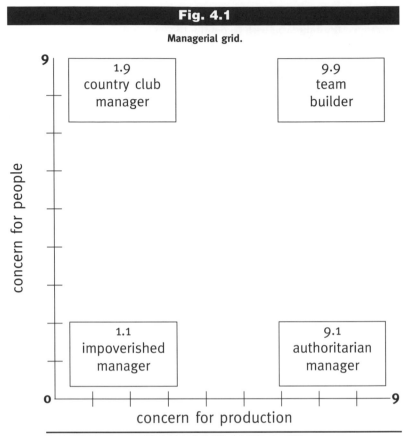

Fig. 4.1

Managerial grid.

Adapted from R. R. Blake & J. S. Mouton, 1966.

people and high production style as 'team' or 'democratic' management. The implication is that managers should focus equally on people and production, and that this is the best style of leadership for almost all business situations.

However, if you look at the scenario at the beginning of the chapter, the young club manager, Paul, decided not to consult with other managers or staff but to act in an autocratic way. This often happens in an emergency situation.

Situational theories

These theories work on the assumption that different styles of leadership are required in different situations and with different people.

Style and the work situation

Researchers from this school of thought have looked at some of the different factors that influence leadership behaviour. Fiedler (1974), for example, studied the quality of leader-member relations (if a manager gets along well with the group he does not have to rely on formal authority), task structure (if tasks are highly structured this calls for a directive approach) and, finally, position power. These three factors — interpersonal relationships, task structure and position power — were then matched to various leadership situations to ascertain which styles of leadership would be most suitable.

Style and the job maturity of employees

Other theorists, Paul Hersey and Kenneth Blanchard (1977) pointed out that the 'maturity' of the staff determined the style of leadership. When staff are new to the job, they need a lot of direction. Once they have learned the basics of the job they need support in forming relationships with the rest of the team. As the person learns more about the job, less support is needed and independence grows. With the 'mature' employee, task and people orientation can both be low, freeing the manager to spend time with more recent employees. A simplified version of Hersey and Blanchard's model is illustrated in Fig. 4.2.

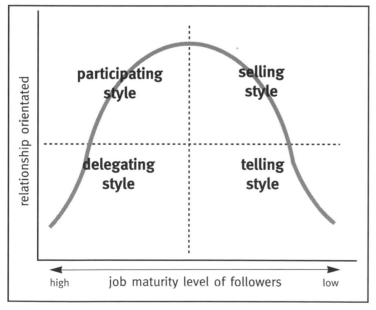

Fig. 4.2

Job maturity model.

Adapted from P. Hersey & K. Blanchard (1977).

In organisations in which staff turnover is high (and this is certainly the case in the hospitality industry where turnover rates for casuals in hotels, for example, can be as severe as 200 per cent for casual staff and 70 per cent for permanent staff in one year) there are implications for the style of leadership required. In terms of this model, most new employees would need high levels of both task and relationship support. Independent, 'mature' employees needing little support and direction would be rare indeed in organisations with such a high staff turnover.

Fig. 4.3

Mind map — a personal theory of leadership.

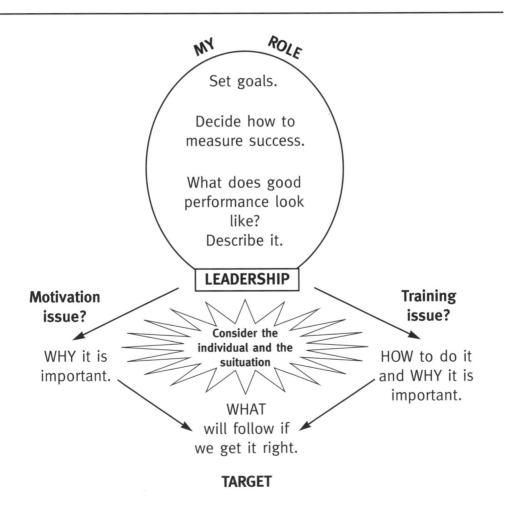

Other situational approaches

There are a number of other situational approaches. One that is sometimes used requires managers to answer a number of 'yes' and 'no' questions to determine the most appropriate leadership style for a range of different situations. The cynic might suggest that this process could be programmed so that managers could resort to computer-aided leadership style choice (CALSC). Entertaining as this thought might be, it confirms an idea with which most people are very comfortable: leadership is a complex thing requiring considerable judgement. Leadership should be a process of action learning during which leadership skills are tested and ideas on leadership are further developed in the light of the outcome of these experiences.

Your own theory of leadership

As someone in charge of others, you need to have a plan for how you will approach the issue of leadership. In the mind map illustrated in Fig. 4.3, a supervisor has developed his own ideas about the topic. As his experience as a supervisor and manager grows he may have to revise his ideas. However, this is a good starting point for a personal action theory of leadership which is ready to be tested and refined.

Discussion questions

1 *Choose three leaders (from either business, sport, education or politics) and compare their personality traits.*
2 *Explain what Blake and Mouton mean by 'country club leadership'.*
3 *Develop a list of crisis situations that could develop in your industry and describe the most appropriate leadership style for handling each of them effectively.*
4 *People change their leadership style over a period of time, from the time when they are first promoted to the job of supervisor to when they are in senior management roles. Discuss this proposition.*
5 *Describe your personal leadership theory and illustrate it with a diagram.*
6 *Apply and evaluate your personal leadership theory.*

SUMMARY

Good leadership is vital for all managers and supervisors regardless of the industry in which they are working. The primary role of supervisors and frontline managers is to harness the energy and skills of their staff to perform specific work-related tasks effectively and efficiently. During the last few decades, leadership has been the subject of a vast amount of research. The early researchers looked at the personal qualities and behaviours that made good leaders. However, little consistency emerged and other theorists moved on to look at the many variables that influence leaders and their choice of leadership style. Some writers argue that leadership styles are difficult to modify and that leaders should be matched to the most appropriate situations for their particular style. Others suggest that leaders need to be flexible, adapting their style of leadership to the situation and the person they are dealing with.

Case study

Sparks would fly every time there was a meeting of executive housekeepers from the different hotels, particularly between Frieda and Consuela. Frieda was a legend. She had been with the company for 12 years and had worked her way up the housekeeping hierarchy to become a domineering, no-nonsense manager. She told the others that her style was not negotiable. She was working with a group of low-level, low-skilled employees from a wide range of cultural backgrounds who had no career aspirations. She accepted that staff turnover would always be high in the housekeeping department and insisted that this should be taken into account when dealing with staff. She said that she needed to be tough and task orientated — she and her staff were there to get the job done and not to socialise. They all had families to go home to. Consuela, on the other hand, was an ex-school teacher and a people-focused person. She and Frieda had major discussions about 'team building' and providing support for staff self-development. Frieda always told Consuela she was wasting her time. Housekeeping was too busy, with too much pressure, to suit anything but an autocratic style.

Whose approach do you favour, Frieda's or Consuela's? Explain why, using some of the theoretical concepts introduced in this chapter.

Given that most tourism and hospitality operations have certain periods in which work pressures are extremely high, how do you think that this should be taken into account by supervisors when thinking about their leadership style?

CHAPTER FIVE

staffing

I'LL NEVER FORGET ONE OF MY ASSIGNMENTS AT COLLEGE COMING back to me with the teacher's comment, 'Call me when you turn 30 and tell me why you are suddenly unemployable'. She was commenting on my advertisement which required applicants to be between 18 and 30. The one word she stressed during the course was 'relevance'. When we planned for interviews we had to prepare interview questions that were relevant to the job. We also had to check job-related knowledge and conduct relevant skills tests. It taught me an invaluable lesson — unless the job interview is carefully planned it is one of the most useless ways of hiring staff.

Now that I'm in charge of a small restaurant, I first screen applicants on the phone and then I ask them to come in for a skills test. They have to come dressed in standard industry uniform (black and whites), open a bottle of wine and carry four plates. When you ask people to come in uniform, this eliminates half the applicants! Those who succeed in the skills test are interviewed. While in the past we spent lots of time answering the phone and interviewing, we have cut this right down and the staff we select stay with us. Now that I'm 31, I have to agree that age has nothing to do with one's ability to do the job! So you don't have to be young to work in our restaurant.

D iscrimination on the grounds of sex, race, age, marital status, sexuality and disability is against the law. This seems contradictory since the process of selecting staff is a process of discriminating between candidates. However, the selection process should be based on **factors that are relevant** to

On completion of this chapter you will be able to:

- **develop plans for staff recruitment**
- **write a job description and person specification**
- **conduct an employment interview and skills test**
- **select staff**
- **plan an induction program**
- **calculate the costs of staff turnover.**

employment in the specific role. As the supervisor above discovered, age was not a factor on which she should be basing selection decisions. Relevant selection criteria include things like relevant work experience, relevant knowledge, specific skills associated with the job, reliability, good teamwork and customer awareness.

This supervisor also discovered that selecting staff could be a very time-consuming process. If each interview took half an hour, and you interviewed a number of candidates, you would not have time to do your normal day's work. Unfortunately this time element causes many supervisors to limit their recruitment efforts to asking staff if they have any friends they think might be suitable for the job!

In this chapter the importance of attracting and selecting the right staff will be discussed.

Identifying recruitment needs

A crucial role of the supervisor is to ensure that enough staff are on duty to cope with the level of business anticipated. At the same time, labour cost must be minimised as it is one of the largest expenditures incurred in running a hospitality operation. From this we can see that one of the most difficult situations faced by today's supervisor is ensuring adequate staffing at the lowest possible cost.

An important strategy for achieving this is to carefully analyse projected business in order to choose the best staffing mix, which generally involves both full-time and casual staff. This will be discussed in more detail in Chapter 11. For the moment, decisions must be made about the people to be hired. Are they to be highly skilled, full-time staff committed to career development, or relatively unskilled staff who are working on a casual basis to earn some extra income? There are definite benefits associated with full-time staff — they are generally more efficient and provide better service, thus earning higher revenue for the business. Casual staff, on the other hand, are more flexible and their labour costs are easier to manage. However many are untrained and lack commitment.

Job design and allocation of duties are considerations, too. Where jobs are simple and require little training, employment of casual labour can be justified. Where considerable training investment is being made, clearly full-time employment should be offered. The role of the supervisor is therefore to look at the short-term labour needs of the organisation and to recruit enough employees with the right skills to staff the business adequately.

Employment legislation

When deciding to employ staff, working conditions (which are spelled out in Awards and Agreements) need to be considered. New employees should be told about pay rates, minimum hours, meal breaks and other conditions of their employment which are outlined in such documents. Without a detailed knowledge of the conditions of employment, a supervisor cannot plan adequately or inform new staff properly.

Equal Employment Opportunity (EEO) and Affirmative Action legislation also needs to be considered in the recruitment and selection processes.

Writing job descriptions and person specifications

Job descriptions describe the duties that an employee performs. A job description for a storeperson is illustrated in Fig. 5.1. These documents are used for a number of purposes which include:

- deciding on the knowledge, experience and other personal attributes required to perform the duties specified
- assisting with the development of advertisements and other recruitment strategies
- allowing new staff to understand the requirements of their jobs
- allowing new staff to develop accurate expectations of their jobs
- identifying training needs
- allowing supervisors to monitor performance
- managing discipline and dismissal where performance is below standard.

The job description helps to ensure that everyone is clear about their expectations. It assists the supervisor and staff member to start off on the right footing.

Looking at Fig. 5.1, you will notice that the job description also lists the conditions of employment. It is most important that these are described in the interview. Anecdotal evidence shows that over 60 per cent of young employees start jobs not knowing what the pay rate will be. Their employers make the assumption that they know the award rates, and the applicants are often too nervous to ask about pay and other conditions of employment. Explaining all aspects of the job during the interview (or providing the applicant with a copy of the job description) is one way of ensuring that new employees are clear about their commitment and will not leave soon after starting.

Note that all duties start with an action word, such as 'assist', 'check' or 'maintain'. As you can see, this job description spells out the requirements of the job very well and a new employee would be very clear about what duties they had to perform. Of course most new staff would be more interested initially in the pay and conditions of employment.

If you were a supervisor looking for a new storeperson, you might discover that you had an experienced candidate in mind but the candidate had no hospitality industry experience, particularly in regard to Occupational Health and Safety and food handling

Fig. 5.1

Sample job description for a storeperson.

Job Description

Position Title: **Storeperson Grade 3**
Reports to: Purchasing Manager
Job Summary: Responsible for receiving and storing general and perishable goods, operating mechanical equipment, implementing quality and financial controls. Responsible for preparing and reconciling reports on stock levels and stock movements.

Duties: Receive and check incoming goods against specifications.
Store goods according to guidelines.
Rotate goods to avoid spoilage.
Maintain cleanliness and neatness of store.
Maintain bin labels.
Maintain accurate records of stock movements.
Anticipate hotel requirements to ensure stock levels are maintained.
Issue stock against correctly completed store requisitions.
Assist with physical inventory counts.
Adhere to Occupational Health and Safety guidelines, particularly in relation to lifting and carrying.
Establish harmonious relationships with other departments, external suppliers and fellow employees.

Conditions: Accommodation, Hotels, Resorts and Gaming Award, 1995.
Storeperson Grade 3, Level 4 — Minimum rate $441.20 pw.
Shift and weekend work, public holidays. Rotating shifts 7 am – 3 pm; 3 pm – 11 pm.

hygiene. This is why the next document, a person specification, is useful. The person specification describes the skills, knowledge and other attributes required for the job. A sample of a person specification (also known as a job specification) is provided in Fig. 5.2. This describes the ideal candidate for the job. If the ideal candidate is not available, it allows for a close match, leaving some skills and knowledge for future training.

Another job description and matching person specification are

Fig. 5.2

Sample person specification (or job specification) for a storeperson.

Person Specification

Position Title: **Storeperson Grade 3**

Job Summary: Responsible for receiving and storing general and perishable goods, operating mechanical equipment, implementing quality and financial controls. Responsible for preparing and reconciling reports on stock levels and stock movements.

Skills: Operation of inventory control software PMS29
Operation of mechanical lifting equipment
Mathematical skills for counting and adding
Ability to check accuracy of documents/ invoices/reports
Neat handwriting
Clear verbal and written communication skills
Ability to prepare simple reports

Knowledge: Bin card systems
Quality of perishable goods
Stock rotation
Stock storage techniques
Occupational Health and Safety (particularly lifting and carrying)
Food Act
Hygienic food handling and storage

Other Attributes: Accuracy
Attention to detail
Honesty
Reliability
Initiative

Essential Requirement: Lifting — see code for manual handling

shown in Figs 5.3 and 5.4, this time for a housekeeping attendant. Once again these documents form an important part of planning for recruitment and selection of new staff.

On reading both person specifications, which list all the qualities

Fig. 5.3

Sample job description for a housekeeping attendant.

Job Description

Position Title: **Housekeeping Attendant**
Reports to: Housekeeping Supervisor
Job Summary: Responsible for room cleaning, replenishment of guest supplies, reporting problems to maintenance or security and customer relations. Key roles are maintaining high standards of cleanliness and presentation and providing quality customer service. Thirteen to 14 rooms per day, 30 minutes per room, plus other cleaning duties as allocated.

Duties: Pick up daily report for rooms allocated.
Sign out keys.
Check with supervisor for priorities.
Prepare housekeeping trolley with supplies and linen.
Enter guest room after knocking.
Clean rooms according to hotel specifications.
Report maintenance defects.
Complete room reports and notify housekeeping supervisor immediately after cleaning.
Greet guests and provide information where requested.
Log lost property with supervisor.
Observe Occupational Health and Safety guidelines.
Report suspicious and other incidents to security.
Carry out other duties as requested.

Conditions of Emploment: Accommodation, Hotels, Resorts and Gaming Award, 1995
Guest Service Grade 2, Level 2 — Minimum rate $391.20 pw.
Weekend work, public holidays. Hours 7 am – 3 pm.

Fig. 5.4

Sample person specification (or job specification) for a housekeeping attendant.

Person Specification

Position Title: **Housekeeping Attendant**

Job Summary: Responsible for room cleaning, replenishment of guest supplies, reporting problems to maintenance or security and customer relations. Key roles are maintaining high standards of cleanliness and presentation and providing quality customer service. Thirteen to 14 rooms per day, 30 minutes per room, plus other cleaning duties as allocated.

Skills: Bed making
Cleaning
Vacuuming
Dusting
Setting VCR/TV
Communicating in English with staff and customers (verbal)

Knowledge: Hotel — services and outlets
Local area — attractions and shopping
Occupational Health and Safety (chemicals, lifting)

Other Attributes: High level fitness
Attention to detail
Reliability
Flexibility (shiftwork)

Desirable: Japanese, Korean, Cantonese (fluent or conversational)

of the ideal person for the job, it becomes evident that few applicants would have all the requirements. If they did not, training would be required. For example, a storeperson who had worked for a retail chain might have very limited food knowledge, especially in terms of hygienic food-handling practices. Likewise, a housekeeping attendant might need to be trained in guest relations, especially in providing hotel information.

Recruiting staff

Once the job description and person specification have been developed, they can be used to prepare an advertisement. There are a number of ways in which this material can be used:

- offering opportunities to internal staff
- providing career guidance information for casual applicants
- referring jobs to placement agencies
- informing college students of the job
- advertising in newspapers
- advertising on the internet.

The advertisement needs to maintain a careful balance between encouraging people to apply and limiting applicants to those who have the desired skills. This balance is also influenced by labour market factors. If, for example, you were advertising for a chef, you would know that your advertisement would be one of many, and that chefs are hard to find. For this reason your advertisement would have to be very eye-catching and positive. On the other hand, being too positive and not discriminatory enough can lead to terrible headaches. This occurred when an American restaurant advertised for staff and attracted applicants in the thousands for fewer than 50 positions. If requirements for experience or food and beverage service skills had been included in the advertisement, it would have limited the number of applicants. A similar situation occurred when a large chain advertised for managers without stipulating the necessity for experience in management or hospitality.

The balance we are talking about is illustrated in Fig. 5.5. In this diagram, the positive nature of the job advertised outweighs the skill requirements. In many advertisements, however, there is nothing to encourage a person to apply, the potential applicant being presented with a discouraging list of minimum requirements. The response to this type of advertisement would be low.

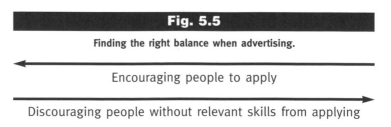

Fig. 5.5
Finding the right balance when advertising.

Encouraging people to apply

Discouraging people without relevant skills from applying

In the advertisement for a housekeeping attendant in Fig. 5.6, the job description and person specification in Figs 5.3 and 5.4 have been used to summarise the key features of the job and the minimum requirements.

Fig. 5.6

Sample advertisement for housekeeping attendants.

Galah Plaza

The Galah Plaza is a busy four star hotel which attracts large numbers of tour groups, mainly from Asian tourism markets. It requires the following staff:

HOUSEKEEPING ATTENDANTS

Housekeeping attendants are responsible for room cleaning, replenishment of guest supplies, reporting maintenance problems and providing quality service to our guests. Staff who work in our Housekeeping Department give the following reasons for enjoying their work:

- Training and support is provided for all new staff.
- Career development is possible within the department.
- Transfers to other departments are encouraged after a minimum period.
- The hours are compatible with family commitments.
- The department has excellent team spirit.
- Guests sometimes leave tips.

To apply for the position you need to be able to work from 7 am to 3 pm on a roster which includes weekend work and public holidays. Experience in cleaning and customer relations is required. The ability to speak an Asian language would be advantageous but is not essential. We need energetic and reliable staff who are eager to join one of the best housekeeping teams in the city.

Please contact Jennifer Wong between 9 am and 1 pm, Monday to Friday.

Galah Plaza

22 Kenthurst Street Adelaide 5000. Tel. (08) 8246 0050.

Fig. 5.7

Selection process.

ADVERTISEMENT

TELEPHONE CALLS

RÉSUMÉ/APPLICATION FORM

INTERVIEW

SKILLS TEST

Selecting staff

The next step is to select staff. The screening process has often already begun by specifying the minimum requirements in the advertisement. These requirements should be addressed again when an applicant telephones since some are overly optimistic. For example, although an advertisement might say that the applicant must be over 18 (to serve alcohol), it is quite probable that a few enthusiastic 17-year-olds might apply. The screening process can then move on to the next stage which involves looking at the personís details in the résumé or application form. Only then should interviews or skills tests be conducted since they are very time consuming. The selection process is illustrated in Fig. 5.7.

Each stage should eliminate the least suitable applicants and, of course, if only a few applicants applied, you would move more quickly and compress the stages.

Planning induction programs

Induction is the process of settling the new employee into their new position. According to most accounts, this is something that few tourism and hospitality operations do successfully. Most new staff are thrown in during busy service periods and are expected to find their feet quickly. Research shows that early impressions are long lasting and influence the person's attitude to the job for longer than might be expected. The new person's levels of skill and motivation are also important from a customer service viewpoint and, in addition, a new employee needs to be aware of their responsibilities. In this industry some of the most important of these are:

• requirements of liquor legislation, including responsible service of alcohol
• requirements of food legislation, including hygienic food handling
• emergency procedures and accident prevention (Occupational Health and Safety).

Some serious accidents have occurred in hospitality operations, including electrocution, burns and hold-ups. If you were the supervisor of a 15-year-old involved in such an incident you would want to be able to show that you had trained your staff member in the correct work procedures for such situations. The necessity for checklists to ensure that everyone is given the required information is shown in Fig. 5.8. The new employee also needs time to adjust to

Fig. 5.8

Induction checklist.

Week One	
Topics for Induction	**Yes or No**
I have been taken on a tour of the establishment.	
I have been taken on a detailed tour of the department.	
I have been introduced to my work colleagues.	
I have been told how to sign on when arriving.	
I have had meal breaks explained and have visited the staff canteen.	
I know what to do if I need to leave my work area.	
I have been told about the company's general philosophy and approach to customers.	
I have been told about some of the regular customers, their names and their usual orders.	
I have been given a copy of my job description.	
I have been told about my conditions of employment, including probation, leave and notice.	
I have had my pay and deductions explained and have filled out the necessary tax forms.	
I know what to do in an emergency.	
My on-job training has started and is progressing at a satisfactory rate.	
I know where to go if I need assistance.	
I have the following questions after my first week:	
Signature Employee: Date:	
Signature Supervisor: Date:	

the new workplace culture and someone should be assigned to him or her to ensure that this transition is as easy and positive as possible.

This type of checklist is invaluable because it ensures that each employee is given all the necessary information. It demonstrates to the new person that their induction period is important. In addition, asking them to take care of the checklist allows them to take part of the responsibility for their learning.

During the following weeks supervisors should cover other things in more detail since not all information could be given to the person on the first day. For example, the new employee would need to know about some of the following additional subjects:

- accident prevention
- Occupational Health and Safety Committees
- reporting accidents
- Workers' Compensation claims
- emergency procedures (in case of fires, bomb scares, hold-ups and first aid, for example)
- policies relating to Equal Employment Opportunity
- sexual harassment and grievance procedures
- Affirmative Action
- organisational aims and objectives
- quality standards
- performance appraisal
- training and career development
- transfer and promotion
- counselling
- dismissal procedures.

Providing new staff with an employee handbook gives them written information on company policy, however the supervisor should take the time to discuss each of the topics with new employees. Larger organisations often have formal sessions (often known as orientation sessions) which are addressed by senior management. Many of the above topics would be covered at such sessions.

Looking back at the induction checklist, you will note that the employee is required to sign this document to say that he or she has been given the required information. This practice is particularly useful where the new employee is very young, as they often are in the hospitality industry. Many supervisors feel a greater than usual responsibility for them and want to ensure that unnecessary accidents do not happen.

A careful induction process can also help new staff settle into the job. There are too many stories in the industry of groups of new staff starting jobs and up to 40 per cent of them leaving before the end of the first month. This high turnover is costly as the next section will demonstrate.

Calculating the cost of staff turnover

There are a number of visible and invisible costs associated with staff turnover. Some of the more visible costs include:

- advertising
- overtime to replace staff who leave
- time taken in interviewing and selecting new staff
- time taken training new staff
- payroll and administrative costs.

Some of the invisible costs include:

- loss of business because service is slow
- loss of business because the organisation's reputation is damaged
- increased stress levels and low morale of remaining staff
- increased waste
- increased workplace accidents.

As a minimum, most employers would agree that it costs at least $1000 to employ, induct and train a new employee. Estimates range, in fact, from $2000 to $4000 for entry level staff. At higher levels the costs are, of course, even more significant. For everyone's sake it is therefore essential that the supervisor make good selection decisions, ensuring that the new employee is clear about expectations and that the first few days and weeks in the job flow as smoothly as possible. Experienced, well-trained staff with high morale provide good service. This type of service is efficient and positive, and leads

Fig. 5.9

Positive staffing dynamic.

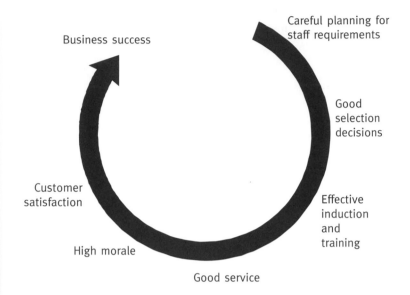

● ● ● ● ● ● ● ● ● ● ● ● ● ● ● ● ● ●

SUMMARY

In this chapter we have dealt with the issue of staffing, in particular the role of the supervisor in making sure that sufficient trained staff are on duty to provide good service. This would be easy if supervisors were given unlimited staffing budgets, but they are not, and labour costs are watched carefully by management. For this reason, careful planning for staff requirements, sensible recruitment and selection, well-monitored induction and training programs, and concern for the new employee's morale and career development are all part of the supervisor's challenging role. Where staff turnover is kept as low as possible through carefully developed and implemented strategies, the supervisor's role in staffing is made much easier, and customer service and business will improve as a result.

● ● ● ● ● ● ● ● ● ● ● ● ● ● ● ● ● ●

to higher levels of customer satisfaction and more business. This positive cycle is illustrated in Fig. 5.9.

Discussion questions

1 *Ethnic restaurants are exempt from Anti-Discrimination legislation if they wish to employ 'authentic' staff. Do you agree or disagree with this approach?*

2 *What sorts of skills tests could you use for staff working as kitchen hands, room attendants or telephone operators? Design appropriate observation checklists in order to compare candidates.*

3 *What are the positives and negatives associated with employing casual staff (look at this from a management and an employee point of view)?*

4 *Staff shortages, poor training and high stress levels are just some of the aspects of a negative staffing cycle. Draw a cycle opposite to that illustrated in Fig. 5.9 and discuss how a hospitality establishment can move from a negative to a positive cycle.*

Case study

As a new supervisor you notice that there seem to be too many casual staff changing shifts after very short working hours. This leads to confusion and mistakes. Many of the employees seem to be inexperienced and some appear to be downright unhappy. You have to deal with numerous complaints from customers.

Develop a step-by-step proposal for the manager of the operation to improve morale and service, starting with the design of job descriptions for staff. Prepare a sample to show her when you discuss your proposal. Bear in mind that she is a great believer in the KIS principle — keep it simple.

CHAPTER SIX

training and
assessment

On completion of this chapter you will be able to:

- **plan for and document one-to-one training sessions**
- **arrange locations and resources**
- **prepare for and conduct training sessions**
- **assess the success of training**
- **evaluate and follow up training.**

WE HAD A JUNIOR WORKING AT THE AGENCY. SHE SENT A COUPLE ON a holiday which did not turn out well and the couple sued the company when they returned under the Trade Practices Act. They said that their expectations had not been met. Some of the photographs in the advertising material were shown in court and compared with their holiday shots of the places where they had stayed. Unfortunately she had not explained to them that the highly discounted rates were for the less attractive rooms at most of the locations. For example, in one hotel the view from the room was a back alley, whereas the advertising shots had been taken from the terrace on the roof. Unfortunately she was not trained or experienced in these things and I felt really sorry for her, making such a poor start to her career. The rest of us know that you need to explain these things fully to clients and to make sure they understand why they are getting the discounted rates. Travelling up north in the rainy season is a good example — clients need to know that it could rain for days and they might not see the brochure-type scenery. You have to know your products and give as much information as possible so the client has clear expectations. This only comes with training.

This new employee had not received sufficient information during training, particularly about the importance of advising clients on every detail of their journeys. This, together with some basic information on Trade Practices law, would have helped her to understand why this level of detail is so crucial. In the same way, knowledge of food poisoning and its causes can help employees understand why some procedures in the kitchen are so important. Once again, these procedures have a legislative basis in the Food Act. In many cases, there are good reasons why policies and procedures are put in place and they form a key part of training.

Identifying the need for training

The previous chapter mentioned the 'gap' between the job requirements (expressed in the job description) and the person recruited for the role. Where such a gap exists training is clearly necessary. This is illustrated in Fig. 6.1. Of course some staff start with no experience at all and the training required is extensive. As a supervisor, your first step is to identify training needs. This is possible by looking at the duties to be performed and analysing the skill, knowledge and attitude requirements, as we did in the last chapter. In some situations, however, supervisors are told that there is a training need when this is not the case. For example, you may be informed that your staff need training in customer relations but, on reflection, you might realise that they are adequately trained but poorly motivated. Or there may be other reasons for unsatisfactory performance, such as understaffing, lack of essential resources or group conflict. Careful analysis is therefore necessary before concluding that training is the solution to the problem.

WE'VE HAD this sort of thing before, but you have to worry about how Games visitors will view it. Beverley and Peter Horne, of Penrith, at a local restaurant, ordered their meal and a half-bottle of red wine (total of $88.20), and oh, could they each have a glass of water?

NO, said the waitress, it's against the management's principles — they could buy bottled water. There were spare glasses on the table, so they took them to the customers' toilets and filled them from the wash-basin taps. The waitress was horrified, so when a request for a refill was refused, they went and filled the glasses again. They told her that in the United States each table had a jug of iced water. 'This isn't America', was the icy reply.

Column 8, *Sydney Morning Herald*, 29 May 1998.

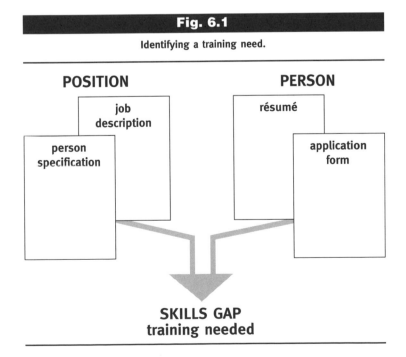

Fig. 6.1

Identifying a training need.

POSITION   PERSON

job description

résumé

person specification

application form

SKILLS GAP
training needed

Four-step training

Once a training need has been identified, careful planning is essential. The following four-step training process has been used for many years and is a reliable formula for training staff at operational level. The four steps are prepare, present, practise and put to work (see Fig. 6.2). These will be described in detail and a training plan used to illustrate how they work.

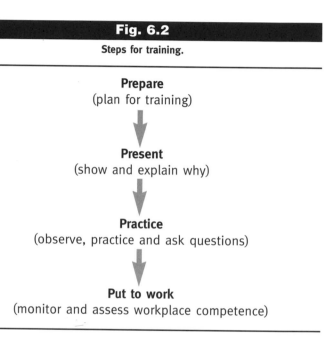

Fig. 6.2
Steps for training.

Prepare
(plan for training)

Present
(show and explain why)

Practice
(observe, practice and ask questions)

Put to work
(monitor and assess workplace competence)

Prepare

Before training commences, a number of things need to be organised, including the location and resources required for the training session. Trainees need to be told what to expect in terms of what they will learn, why it is required, how training will progress and how their performance will be assessed. Any barriers to learning, such as language, need to be identified.

Having done this, you need to think through the training session, taking a systematic approach. Unless training is carefully planned by an experienced person, key information is likely to be forgotten. Imagine the catastrophes — and, in some cases, tragedies — that could occur if employees were not informed of the following:

• Turning a computer off without saving can lose valuable work.

- Cleaning the stove carelessly can lead to gas being turned on by mistake.
- Leaving a puddle on the floor can lead to a nasty accident.
- Peeled potatoes go brown if you don't cover them with water.
- Submerging an electrical appliance in water can cause a fatal accident.

And there is the legendary tragic story of someone dying in a hospital in the same room at the same time every week for several weeks until it was realised that the cleaner was using the power point for the vacuum cleaner and turning off the life support system for half an hour! Her training was clearly rather limited!

Looking at the training plan in Fig. 6.3, you can see how important planning and preparation are for effective training. Key steps and key information have been listed so that the training will be comprehensive. The training is for the seemingly simple task of sandwich-making, however there are interesting aspects to this training such as the combination of ingredients, the use of ingredients that don't make sandwiches go soggy, the careful handling and storing of bread, and the final presentation. If you ran a catering company supplying sandwiches for lunch meetings, you would be assured of more business if your clients were happy with your products. If they were not, they would change caterers without hesitation. We have already seen how a client can withhold further business from a company at the start of this chapter. However, in this case, the poor training also led to bad publicity and legal costs.

Present

The next step in training is 'show and tell'. This involves showing the new trainee what to do logically and slowly, at the same time explaining the reasons why these steps are important. For example, if you leave the bread out for too long, it will curl up and the sandwiches will be very dry. On the other hand, making only one sandwich at a time is very inefficient. All the bread needs to be butttered at once and covered immediately. As you can see from the training plan in Fig. 6.3, food hygiene and safety in knife handling are also vital parts of the training. They involve showing the steps and telling the trainee the reasons why they are important. Unfortunately many supervisors stop their training at this point thinking that the job has been done. However, the next part of training — practice — is the most critical.

Practice

No doubt you have been in a situation in which you have been shown something and then left to do it yourself, feeling quite unsure about what you were doing. The worst examples of this seem to be in computer training where the demonstration is so fast that you can't follow the steps and you are left feeling quite helpless. Every trainer should make sure that the trainee is confident to do the task and then observe their progress. Observation points and questions have been included in the training plan in Fig. 6.3 to give you an example of how to do this effectively. Asking questions helps to check for understanding. By the time the trainee has performed the task and answered the questions, both you, the trainer, and the trainee should be confident that the training has been a success. During the practice session, positive feedback is essential to encourage the trainee. Having planned the training carefully, you are more than able to provide some very specific feedback at this point. For example, you might say, 'By organising your ingredients logically you were able to save valuable time'. This type of feedback is more helpful to a trainee than 'Well done'. Once the practice session is complete it is time to put the person to work.

Fig. 6.3

Training plan for making sandwiches.

Start frame

TRAINING PLAN

Task: Make five platters of sandwiches for a luncheon meeting.

Prepare

1 Arrange time and place for training:

   7.30 am, Wednesday, 4 April

2 Brief employee beforehand:
   Cover task outline, basic hygiene requirements for food handling, timing and outcomes of training.

3 Assemble ingredients and equipment (double quantity for demonstration and practice):

- display cards/standard recipes
- cutting boards
- knives
- platters
- cling wrap
- bread
- butter (room temperature)
- shaved ham
- cheddar cheese (sliced)
- lettuce
- roasted capsicum
- fried eggplant
- boiled eggs
- asparagus (par cooked)
- French mustard
- mayonnaise
- salt
- pepper.

Present (show and tell)

1 Steps

- Wash hands.
- Wash and cut vegetable ingredients.
- Assemble ingredients logically.
- Spread butter on bread.
- Prepare and present sandwiches on platters.
- Cover with cling wrap.
- Store.

2 Explanation

- personal hygiene
- cleanliness of utensils and work area
- quality and freshness of ingredients
- correct handling and washing of ingredients
- safety in knife handling
- uniformity in presentation
- storage and handling of bread
- effective taste and colour combinations
- attractiveness of food presentation
- storage of final product.

Practice (watch)

1 Observation points — process

- hygienic work practices
- safe work practices (especially knife handling)
- reduction of waste
- managing workflow
- problem-solving.

2 Observation points — product

- freshness
- uniformity
- presentation
- taste.

3 Questions

- Why is it important to have a clean chopping board and knife?
- Why should you wash some ingredients?
- What is the best temperature for butter?
- Why is it important to work quickly to cut, prepare and store sandwiches?
- What are some alternative ingredients you could use if there were no lettuce?
- How can you avoid sandwiches becoming soggy?
- Which aspects of presentation do you pay attention to?

Put to work

1 Follow-up items for observation:

- managing workflow — **speed** in preparation and assembling of ingredients, efficient workflow
- **hygienic** work practices
- **safe** work practices, especially knife skills when working quickly
- **presentation** and freshness of final product
- flair and innovation.

2 Follow-up questions:

- Why is it important to plan and prepare ingredients beforehand?

- How could food poisoning occur as a result of contamination in sandwich preparation?
- Why is timing and storage so important in preparing sandwiches?
- Explain the nutritional value of the ingredients you are using.

End frame

Put to work

Learning comes with repetition, and in jobs where speed is important this develops over time. As you can see, the training plan takes this into account by listing observation points and questions to be asked once the trainee has carried out the task a number of times. In this way the supervisor can evaluate whether the training has been successful in the long term and whether the trainee is competent. As you can see from the task illustrated in Fig. 6.3, the emphasis is now on speed, managing workflow and problem-solving. At this stage you are actually assessing whether training has been a success. You are, in fact, assessing workplace competence. The training and assessment phases are illustrated in Fig. 6.4.

Fig. 6.4

Assessment of learning and workplace competence.

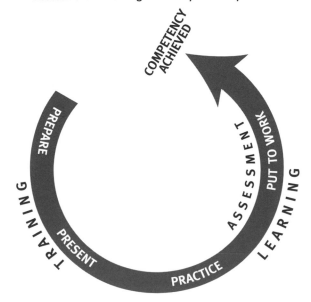

Competency standards

In the hospitality industry 'competency standards' form the basis for training and assessment. This is illustrated in Fig. 6.5 where the performance of a kitchen trainee preparing for service is described. As you can see, if the trainee had acquired all the skills and knowledge described in the training plan in Fig. 6.3, they could be assessed as competent in elements 1, 2 and 3. Only element 4 (preparing meat and seafood) would not have been assessed in the performance of the task of sandwich-making.

Fig. 6.5

Competency standards — an example.

Unit: Organise and Prepare Food

Unit descriptor: This unit deals with the skills and knowledge required to organise and prepare foodstuffs for the kitchen.

Element 1 Prepare equipment for use.	Performance criteria • Ensure that equipment is clean before use, is the correct type and size and is safely assembled and ready for use.
Element 2 Assemble and prepare ingredients for menu items.	Performance criteria • Ingredients are identified correctly, according to standard recipes. • Ingredients are the correct quantity, type and quality and are assembled and prepared in required form and time frame.
Element 3 Prepare dairy, dry goods, fruit and vegetables.	Performance criteria • Food is prepared according to weight, amount and/or number of portions, including: • Vegetables and fruit are cleaned, peeled and/or prepared as required for menu items. • Dairy products are correctly handled and prepared as required for menu items. • Dry goods are measured, sifted where appropriate and used as required for menu items. • General food preparation as required for menu items. This could include but is not limited to sandwiches, garnishes, batters and coatings.

Element 4
Prepare meat, seafood and poultry.
	Performance criteria
	• Food is prepared and portioned according to size and/or weight in the following ways:
	  • Meat is trimmed, minced or sliced and prepared accordingly.
	  • Fish and seafood are cleaned and prepared and/or filleted correctly.
	  • Poultry is trimmed and prepared correctly.

Range of variables
• This unit applies to all establishments where food is prepared and served.
• The term organising and preparing food is also referred to by the French counterpart 'mise-en-place' and includes:
  • Basic preparation prior to serving food. Whilst it might involve cooking components of a dish, it does not include the actual presentation.
  • The tasks required to make a section of the kitchen ready for service.

Evidence guide
UNDERPINNING SKILLS AND KNOWLEDGE
To demonstrate competence, evidence of skills and knowledge in the following areas is required:
• basic products and types of menus
• hygiene
• occupational health and safety
• logical and time efficient workflow.

CONTEXT OF ASSESSMENT
This unit may be assessed on or off the job, through practical demonstration on the job or in a simulated workplace environment. This should be supported by a range of methods to assess underpinning knowledge.

CRITICAL ASPECTS OF ASSESSMENT
Evidence should include a demonstrated ability to efficiently organise and prepare a general range of foods. The focus of this general range will vary according to the sector in which the kichen operates.

LINKAGES TO OTHER UNITS
It is recommended that this unit be assessed in conjunction with:
• Present Food
• Clean and Maintain Premises

When assessing against these standards, the following questions can be asked to ascertain whether the main principles of assessment have been followed (see also Fig. 6.6):

Validity

The question to be asked here is whether the assessment task reflects the performance described in the competency standards. If, for example, we asked a trainee to write an essay on sandwich-making, this would not be a valid assessment method.

Reliability

The relevant question here is whether the same assessment outcome would occur on another occasion. If another assessor were to use the same observation points and questions, no doubt he or she would reach the same conclusion and the assessment would be reliable. If, on the other hand, one assessor were to assess making one sandwich and another were to assess making five platters, the reliability of the assessment would be in question. The first assessor would have no opportunity to assess speed and workflow. To ensure reliability, assessors need to develop assessment checklists (such as the observation points and questions in the training plan in Fig. 6.3) and discuss assessment outcomes with each other to check consistency.

Sufficiency

The question in this instance is whether the assessor has enough evidence to make a decision. As a general rule it is preferable to have different types of evidence. In our example two assessment methods were used: observation and questioning. These are the most commonly used approaches at the operational level. In addition to them, another useful piece of evidence to support the assessment decision would be the supervisor's report on the person's skills. Certainly, in the example provided, the assessor could not use the task of sandwich-making to assess the whole of the unit, Organise and Prepare Food, because one important element was not covered by the task performed. And, of course, that element, preparing meat, seafood and poultry, was a complex and significant one and had still to be assessed.

Flexibility

When assessing a person's skills in the workplace, it is important to do so in the context of normal workplace practice. For the competency standard outlined in Fig. 6.5, there are a number of tasks a kitchen hand or cook might perform which would enable assessment of the same skills required for 'preparing for service'.

Authenticity and currency

The final questions that need to be asked, especially about written evidence such as references, relate to whether the person's skills and

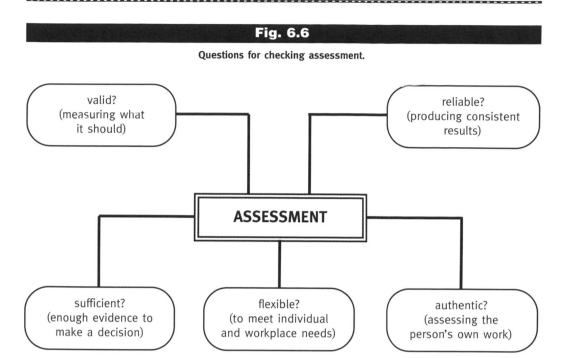

Fig. 6.6

Questions for checking assessment.

valid? (measuring what it should)

reliable? (producing consistent results)

ASSESSMENT

sufficient? (enough evidence to make a decision)

flexible? (to meet individual and workplace needs)

authentic? (assessing the person's own work)

knowledge are current and whether their documents are authentic. This is why references are seldom used as the only source of evidence by an assessor.

Holistic and atomistic assessment

These strange terms have been widely used in recent times. Holistic assessment involves assessing a fairly substantial task which integrates a broad range of skills and knowledge. Atomistic assessment focuses on very minor, isolated tasks, such as slicing one type of vegetable. These are illustrated in Fig. 6.7.

Of course the debate is about how 'holistic' you can get. In general, assessments of novices tend to be fairly atomistic in the early stages of their training, while assessments of experienced employees can be quite holistic. If, for example, a chef who had trained in another country was seeking recognition for a large range of units, the

Fig. 6.7

Atomistic and holistic continuum.

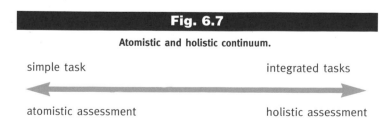

simple task   integrated tasks

atomistic assessment   holistic assessment

assessment task would be far more complex than for sandwich-making. Preparing a range of dishes, using different cooking methods, for a busy dinner period would be an example of a more holistic assessment than the one discussed above. It would include the next unit of competence, which covers various cooking methods.

For supervisors, the most important considerations are whether the task the person performs for assessment reflects the performance described in the competency standards and whether key skills and knowledge have been assessed.

Hospitality industry assessment scheme

The assessment scheme used in the hospitality industry is ACCESS. The scheme involves licensing assessors to conduct workplace assessments of various units of the competency standards (known also as training packages). Information about ACCESS can be obtained from Tourism Training in your state or territory. Since the competency standards form the basis for much of the training conducted in the hospitality industry and in the educational sector, this makes training outcomes portable, which means that achievement against a unit, such as the one illustrated in Fig. 6.5, is transferable from one training provider to another and from one employer to another. The hospitality industry is the flagship for many other industries which are endeavouring to achieve the same portability in training and assessment outcomes as it has attained.

Training and assessment for career paths or qualifications

Since competency standards form the basis for training and assessment in colleges and in the workplace, individuals can acquire units (or modules as they are referred to in colleges) anywhere and use them to build a qualification. This is illustrated in Fig. 6.8 which shows how training and asssessment can be integrated.

Evaluating your training and assessment

As a trainer or assessor, you need to evaluate your own performance on the basis of the following three forms of feedback:

* the performance of the trainee
* feedback from the trainee
* reflection on your own performance.

Fig. 6.8

Using competency standards to integrate training approaches.

National hospitality competency standards (training packages)

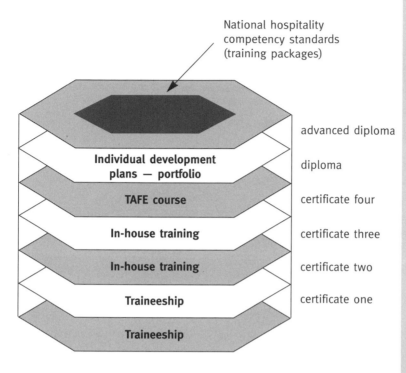

advanced diploma

Individual development plans — portfolio

diploma

TAFE course

certificate four

In-house training

certificate three

In-house training

certificate two

Traineeship

certificate one

Traineeship

SUMMARY

This chapter has covered the four key steps of training: prepare, present, practice and put to work. The practice stage of training is the most important for the trainee. If the trainer has prepared well, demonstrated the main steps and explained why they are important, the trainee's confidence should grow quickly. The final stage of training involves putting the trainee to work and returning later to check on their level of competence. Whether the trainee has reached the performance level described in the appropriate competency standard forms part of the assessment. Evaluating training and assessment is also an important part of the supervisor's role in order to improve their performance in these areas.

From this feedback, you can make adjustments to future training and assessment. For example, you may need to improve your briefing of the trainee, or to slow down when presenting information, or to provide the trainee with better opportunities to practise. Finally, records should be kept on the training and assessment outcomes for the employee's personal file.

Discussion questions

1 *Explain why each of the steps in training is important.*

2 *What are the benefits of having competency standards in the hospitality industry to describe performance?*

3 *Do you prefer to talk about training or learning? What difference does it make?*

4 *Do you think that process (for example, food preparation) and product (for example, menu item) should be assessed? Explain why, giving your own example.*

5 *When do you think a person is ready for assessment?*

6   *In the previous chapter we mentioned a situation in which an experienced storeperson was hired but she had not worked in the hospitality industry and had not dealt with food products. Develop a training plan to ensure that she learns how to handle and store perishable products, emphasising the importance of food hygiene. Use the final stage of the training to conduct a skills and knowledge assessment.*

Case study

After two years working in the bar of a hotel you are promoted to a supervisory position. Your first goal is to improve the level of customer service. Most procedures are followed to the letter, but there is little interaction with customers, most of whom come from overseas. Customer feedback forms have said that the service is efficient but cold. Your aim is to expand the people skills of your staff and to improve communication with your customers.

Develop a training and assessment plan for this initiative so that staff who complete your training and assessment will emerge with competencies that are nationally recognised.

CHAPTER SEVEN

planning and organising
workflow

THE DESIGN OF A BAR IS VERY IMPORTANT. AT THE TUMBAROOMA Hotel we were getting complaints about the service of beer from new customers in the bar. The regulars all sat close to the beer taps which was the main working area of the bar staff. They were therefore served more promptly and were often involved in conversation with the staff. We resolved this by moving the Carlton Cold beer taps to the centre of the bar. We also moved the fridge and installed a bigger dishwaster for the glasses. This speeded up the workflow tremendously. But the most important change we made was to increase storage space so that staff members were not disappearing to fetch stocks during our busy periods.

Workflow problems were solved in this hotel by making changes to the physical work area. No doubt there are many chefs in the industry who would be thrilled by improvement of their work areas — one recently described how he plated food for a large function with the plates spread out on the floor! A more hygienic solution would have been a trolley designed to stack large numbers of plates already garnished and ready for service. However, the importance of workflow planning is never more evident than with room service breakfasts. As you know, eggs need to be served the minute they are prepared, and one hotel's solution to this problem was to install a stove in one of the service elevators. Housekeepers who have to travel up and down tall buildings to fetch supplies also know how important it is to make them more accessible by keeping stores on each floor. Unfortunately, experienced staff are too seldom consulted when the building is designed.

On completion of this chapter you will be able to:
- **discuss the importance of planning workflow**
- **explain and apply a range of time management strategies**
- **apply a range of workflow planning techniques**
- **explain and evaluate the outcomes of workflow planning**
- **develop contingency plans**
- **improve operational efficiency and customer satisfaction.**

In each of these examples, workflow improvement was based on changes to the physical layout of the work area or on improvement in the equipment used. There are many other ways in which workflow can be refined and these generally involve job design. This means planning the tasks staff perform more carefully. To put it more simply, deciding who does what and when. Sometimes training is required to implement new and more efficient approaches. Technology can also assist directly by helping staff to perform tasks, such as relaying orders to the kitchen, or indirectly by speeding the provision of data on service so that workflow planning can be based on reliable information.

Workflow planning

Labour costs in tourism and hospitality are higher than average. As these costs are such a significant part of the cost of goods sold, they need to be managed carefully. This means that good service also needs to be efficient service. To achieve a high level of productivity, managers need to look closely at workflow planning. Improved planning can reduce delays and increase efficiency.

In this chapter we will look at a range of approaches for improving workflow, including job redesign and training.

Work area planning

The physical layout of the work area is tremendously important for many jobs in the tourism and hospitality industry. In the front office, the banquet department, the kitchen and the stores area, the physical layout of the work area can lead to people crossing paths all the time, and to repetitive trips from one end of the section to another. Even where design problems cannot be easily resolved, moving equipment and planning workflow can increase efficiency.

Fig. 7.1 clearly illustrates the difference between good and bad workflow planning in a hotel bathroom. We can see that one approach to workflow planning involves plotting the paths of individuals working in a department and then looking at more efficient ways of working. Moving stock from one area to another, removing physical obstacles, providing improved storage space and improving lighting can all help to make staff more efficient. Anyone who has travelled on a jumbo jet would have observed how carefully the work stations were laid out and how service was carefully synchronised despite the limited space.

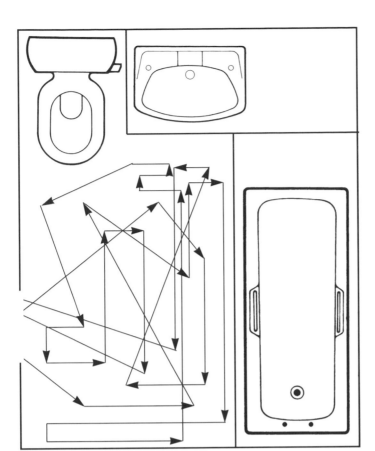

Fig. 7.1

Planned workflow increases efficiency.

Cleaning Bathroom
— Old Method

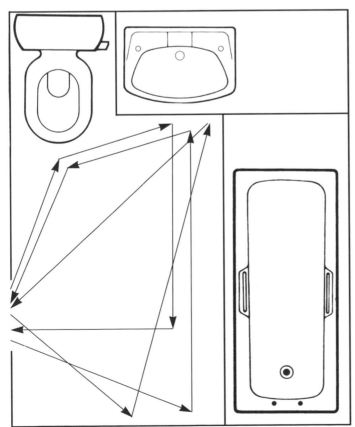

Cleaning Bathroom
— New Method

Job design

In designing the way people carry out their duties it is essential to look at the sequence of duties and the range of tasks performed by different staff members. First let's look at sequencing. Fig. 7.2 illustrates some of the steps involved in opening a bar and restaurant for the day's trading. The sequence of these steps is critical. For example, if the espresso machine is not turned on half and hour before trading you will not be able to make and sell coffee. The same applies to the deep fryer, which takes a long time to heat up. And checking the beer also needs to be performed early in the sequence because if there is a problem with the lines this will need to be checked by the cellar staff.

All of the tasks in Fig. 7.2 would need to be done before checking air-conditioning, preparing garnishes and the many other tasks that need to be performed to prepare for service in a bar and restaurant.

In the front office, also, careful planning is necessary to prepare for the rush at check-out times. What goes on in this department is a very good example of the concept of multiskilling. Where formerly the check-in and check-out desks were quite separate, these days most hotel staff perform both roles. Previously the cashier would have handled all financial transactions — at check-out and during the guest's stay when, for example, they might ask to draw cash electronically. Now a guest service agent performs all tasks associated with arrival and departure. This means that guests are not kept waiting while staff at the other desk are idle.

So far we have discussed the sequence (when) of job design and the allocation of duties to individuals (who). In the following example we will look at the combination of 'what' and 'when' in the

Fig. 7.2

Task sequence — opening bar and restaurant for service.

1 Collect keys and float from food and beverage office.

2 Collect linen from stores area.

3 Unlock doors.

4 Turn on lights and sound system.

5 Turn on deep fryer.

6 Turn on espresso machine after filling with water.

7 Unlock all fridges.

8 Check gas levels for beer and postmix.

9 Pull beer through to check pouring.

performance of a room attendant's job. This position offers a good example of the importance of effective job design because efficiency is quite crucial. Most room attendants are expected to clean a room within 25 minutes. As you can imagine, there is no time to go downstairs for supplies that have been left off the trolley! Unless room cleaning is carefully planned, the room attendant will move constantly to and from the trolley wasting valuable time and effort. Instead, a basket of equipment, including cleaning agents and supplies, should be carried into the bathroom which can then be cleaned systematically, beginning with the toilet. While the sanitising chemicals are at work in the toilet, the bathroom can be cleaned in the most energy-efficient way. And in the bedroom, rather than moving round the bed tucking sheets and blankets in one at a time, the bed linen should be arranged, folded and tucked in at the same time on one side before moving to the other. Such procedures save valuable minutes.

As discussed above, job design can contribute substantially to improvement in workflow. In looking at job design, a supervisor needs to ask the following questions:

- What needs to be done?
- In which order should it be done?
- Who should do it?

This links to the development of job descriptions and preparation for training discussed in the previous two chapters. Job design is illustrated in Fig. 7.3.

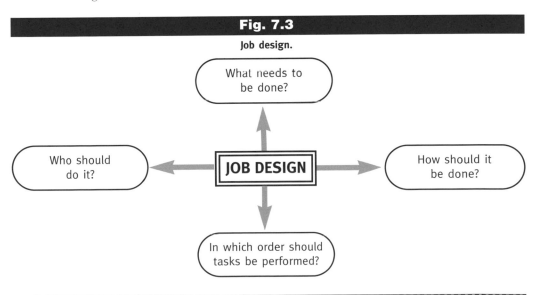

Fig. 7.3

Job design.

Employee input should be used to improve job design and implement changes in the workplace to enhance operational efficiency and customer service. Note that this chapter has not addressed the component, 'How should it be done?' This involves setting standards of performance and monitoring performance, and these topics will be covered in Chapter 8 on delegation and control.

Equipment and technology support

Mechanisation and computerisation have made tremendous inroads into the tourism and hospitality industry. Cook-chill systems, for example, allow hospitals to prepare food in advance which is instantly ready for delivery to the room. This equipment selectively heats some dishes and keeps the rest chilled — all on the same service tray. In restaurants, automatic relay of orders to the kitchen saves time and avoids the necessity for staff to run in and out of the kitchen to deliver handwritten dockets.

The most significant of these developments has been the computerisation of records for future analysis. If you know in advance how many portions of chips you will sell on a rainy public holiday you are well ahead of your competitors. You will have fresh, hot food ready for immediate service and will not waste money on produce that will be discarded. Most importantly, you will know how many staff you will need in the kichen and out the front. This is illustrated in Table 7.1 which shows the projected level of business and actual sales, allowing staff to adequately prepare while maintaining costs at the lowest possible level without compromising service.

Time management

Managing your own time is just as important as managing everyone else's. In this industry, your time often tends to be dictated by circumstantial factors, and many supervisors take on a predominantly trouble-shooting role, stepping in to solve service problems or customer complaints whenever they occur. Unfortunately, unless time is invested in planning for a resolution to many of these problems, such supervisors will lurch from one problem to another without getting on top of anything. There are parts of the day when the job determines your use of time — you need to be on hand during peak periods, for example — but equally there are parts of the day which should be set aside for solving longer term issues and

Table. 7.1

Computerisation has helped to analyse records and project sales.

Fish fillets	12.00	12.30	1.00	1.30	2.00	2.30
Projected sales	5	12	15	3	3	2
Uncooked frozen stock required	80	70	60	50	40	30
Uncooked defrosted stock required	15	15	15	5	5	5
Cooked product	7	13	15	5	5	4
Sold product	6	11	11	8	0	0
Variance (waste)	1	2	4	0	5	4

Comment on day's trading:
Trade slower than same last week, possibly due to Grand Final match on TV. Need to take into account for next year's projection. Sudden demand at 1.30 pm took us by surprise and service was delayed.

making investments in planning. As you have seen from our discussion of the training plan in Chapter 6, and from developing your own, this investment can reap rewards and avoid mistakes (such as poor food handling practices leading to food poisoning).

There are several ways in which you can look at your own time management and these include keeping a log of your activities, using a diary or making other work-scheduling arrangements, maintaining routines and establishing priorities.

Keeping a log

If you keep a log of your daily activities, you are able to analyse how your time is spent and to look at priorities. Such analysis is very useful as it clearly indicates whether time is being wasted on low priority tasks or not.

Keeping a diary

By allocating certain times to certain tasks a supervisor can ensure that each task receives the proper attention. Interviewing new staff is a good example, for the time invested in doing this well pays off in the long term by reducing the amount of time needed for training or problem-solving. If a staff member wants to talk to you, and it is a serious matter, allocate a time and place to discuss the issue thoroughly. A diary is essential for this purpose and it can also be used to record key information from your discussion.

Sticking to routines

One of the most effective ways to manage time is to develop routines. If there is a particular time of day, or a stage in a shift, during which you can work uninterrupted in your office, you will get far more done than if you have a haphazard approach to managing your time.

Establishing priorities

In a busy work schedule it is often impossible to get everything done. As a result some tasks are neglected in the short term. It is essential that the jobs neglected are those which are low priority. Unfortunately the jobs that are most often neglected are the most complex ones because the supervisor doesn't know where to start. As a result there is a tendency to complete simple tasks, such as ordering new aprons, and neglect hard ones, such as developing performance targets for staff and planning training sessions. And there are even more critical tasks that require the time and careful consideration of the supervisor, and they include resolving group conflicts, managing disciplinary issues and improving workplace safety. The general rule is to invest time both in long-term planning and in solving day-to-day problems.

Planning techniques

Setting objectives

One of the simplest ways of improving productivity is to develop targets and then to plan for their achievement. These targets must be achievable. From an employee motivation point of view, staff must be

able to see that their efforts will be rewarded and that there are no obvious hurdles in the way of achieving the desired level of performance. Too often supervisors set targets without removing the hurdles that slow down performance. By consulting staff about workplace changes and goal setting, a supervisor is more likely to win support and motivate staff to achieve the established goals. These goals should be measurable so that staff (and management) can see progress towards their achievement.

An objective is a measurable outcome. It is more specific than a goal, which might be 'to improve customer satisfaction' or 'to increase sales', and can be linked to incentives. Examples of objectives are listed below:

• Increase customer satisfaction ratings by 0.5 per cent.
• Clean guest rooms in 23 minutes on average.
• Increase sales of dessert items by 20 per cent.
• Reduce the cost of breakages by $500.
• Select a new range of 12 menu items within the current price range and introduce the new menu within six weeks.

Fig. 7.4

Chart monitoring decrease in losses and breakages and resultant cost savings.

Losses and Breakages	To Date Last Year	To Date This Year	Amount to Staff Club $
Dinner plates	19	16	18
Bread plates	14	6	32
Cups	20	8	36
Saucers	29	12	61
Bowls	14	15	4
Knives	32	10	23
Forks	20	7	27
Dessertspoons	14	7	15
Teaspoons	56	23	52
Trays	12	4	72
Jugs	3	1	8
			348

Preparing charts

Charts are a valuable way of viewing the current state of affairs and any improvements which occur. Fig. 7.4 illustrates a chart used to monitor breakages and losses of equipment in a hospital. If staff are able to achieve a reduction in breakages and losses to the value of $500, this amount will be allocated to their staff club for their next social function. As you can see, the outcome and cost savings are clearly illustrated by means of this chart.

Fig. 7.5	

Checklist for cleanliness and food handling.

Cleanliness	
rubbish bins	✓
bin and park area	✓
footpath	✓
tables, chairs, counter	✓
floors and windows	✓
menus and displays	✓
Food safety	
products stored correctly	✓
coolroom temperature 0–2 degrees Celsius	✓
freezer –12 to –18 degrees Celsius	✓
all product off the floor	✓
no cross-contamination	✓
door seals close properly	✓
products used correctly — first in, first out	✓

Making checklists

A checklist has already been illustrated in Fig. 7.2. In this, the sequence of tasks to be performed when opening a bar and restaurant for the day's trading was shown, the order of tasks being particularly important. Another checklist which monitors cleanliness and food hygiene is illustrated in Fig. 7.5.

Preparing rosters

Workflow planning is one of the most important considerations when preparing a staff roster. Adequate numbers of staff need to be on duty at all times, particularly during peak periods. Having employees standing around during slow periods is not recommended since the effect this has on the bottom line is disastrous. Preparing staff rosters will be dealt with in more detail in Chapter 11.

Compiling questionnaires

A questionnaire can be used to monitor customer satisfaction, and it can cover a range of factors including staff presentation, speed of service, cleanliness of the establishment, conviviality of the staff and food quality. Although it would appear that only speed of service relates to workflow planning, it is not the only factor. All others would suffer if the 'wheels fell off' during service: for example, problems leading to panic behind the scenes would affect the conviviality of the staff.

Questionnaires can also be used to obtain feedback from staff. This can be more carefully monitored than information obtained in informal meetings.

Using reports

There are a number of reports which can be used by supervisors to improve planning, efficiency and service. Some examples include:

- advance reservations
- check-in and check-out times
- daily revenue (earnings)
- server revenue (takings)
- average customer spend
- menu item popularity
- covers (people served) over time periods
- stock on hand
- stock variances
- absenteeism.

All of these reports provide valuable information which can help with the decision-making process.

Making contingency plans

Sometimes the unexpected happens and when this occurs staff need to be ready for it. For example, your food outlet will probably never experience a hold-up, but if it did it is one of those critical events where lives may be at risk. Contingency plans for a hold-up would involve training staff:

- to keep still and remain calm and quiet
- to obey instructions
- to observe details for indentification
- not to chase the offender or act dangerously
- to call the police
- to seal off the area and ask witnesses to remain.

Having contingency plans for unusual situations is very important as the handling of major incidents can lead to positive, or negative, publicity which can sometimes result in the success or failure of a business.

This important topic will be dealt with further in Chapter 9 on decision-making and problem-solving.

Measuring operational efficiency and customer satisfaction

All of the techniques outlined in this chapter can be used for a 'before and after' analysis of efficiency levels and customer satisfaction. For example, checklists and ratings can be used to observe service skills and timing of service. These observations can be recorded and used to compare with the results of new strategies. In the same way, periodical reports on revenue or sales of particular items can be compared to see whether progress is being made. This is important feedback for a supervisor, and an indicator that quality improvements are occurring. It is also valuable feedback for staff and, linked to rewards, it can lead to new efforts towards improvements in service.

In summary, to plan and organise workflow a supervisor needs to:

- assess the current workload of staff
- schedule work to enhance efficiency and customer service
- prioritise and plan work
- allocate duties
- make changes in consultation with colleagues and staff
- assess outcomes against objectives and agreed timelines.

Discussion questions

1   *If you had an unlimited labour budget you could provide perfect service. Discuss this statement. How can supervisors maximise efficiency while minimising labour costs?*

2   *Why do staff often ignore the objectives set by their supervisors and managers? Explain your ideas in detail and give examples.*

3   *'Sometimes it pays to keep jobs simple, other times you need staff who are multiskilled.' Discuss this statement about job design.*

SUMMARY

In this chapter we have looked at one of the supervisor's most critical roles: planning and organising workflow. In such a high labour cost industry, appropriate scheduling of staff, careful allocation of duties, effective job design and consultation with staff about objectives and timelines are ways in which supervisors can ensure that teams become operationally effective. Supervisors who do not manage work using these methods tend to adopt a trouble-shooting role which could be avoided by investing time in planning, prioritising and resolving longer term issues.

Case study

You know that magic touch that some doctors have when they make you feel like you are their only patient and there is nobody waiting outside? Well, my favourite boss was like that. He always took that little extra time and gave you his full attention. You felt like he was really listening to you and taking notice of what you were saying. The staff adored and trusted him. He often just said, 'What's up?', and that way he solved lots of problems before they occurred. Some bosses I have had are always in a rush, and never have time to stop and listen. You want to see them, but they don't even have time to make eye contact. Fidget, fidget, so many problems to solve! If only they realised that all they do is solve short-term problems and never stop to sort out the long-term ones. Let me give you an example. In my current job at the Waterloo we get very frustrated because the dishwasher is too small and too slow to cope with the number of glasses we go through on a busy night. As a result we do several things, such as using the wrong glasses for the drinks, washing by hand or 'borrowing' glasses from another department. All of this is time consuming and slows down the service. I have tried to tell Dena about this and she has done nothing about it — she can't even stop to listen to the problem. It's all panic and no planning in our department. We never have the right par stock, the closing staff doesn't clean up properly . . . there are so many problems.

Suggest a step-by-step process for Dena including at least the following:

- one way to measure current operational efficiency
- one way to measure current levels of customer satisfaction
- two ways to involve staff in workflow planning
- one way for Dena to manage her own time more effectively
- at least three approaches for improving operational efficiency and/or customer satisfaction
- one way to measure improvement in operational efficiency and/or customer satisfaction and to provide feedback to staff.

CHAPTER EIGHT

delegation and
control

THE PLACE WAS COMPLETELY DEVOID OF PROFESSIONALISM AND ethics. The establishment was located in the ski fields and the staff were all there just for the season — from the manager down. The manager had absolutely no idea, he was there for only one reason — skiing. As a result, the staff were left to do their own thing. One minute they would be serving behind the bar, the next minute they would be on the other side of the bar drinking free drinks supplied by their colleagues. There was no effort to control waste so the chef ordered in huge quantities of supplies and then distributed the leftovers to the staff. Sometimes housekeeping staff wouldn't even change the linen between guests! Everyone knew that there was no supervision and if the worst came to the worst there were lots of other jobs at the snow. All the places were desperate for staff.

A supervisor's most common task is giving orders. Clearly in this example the supervisors and manager were disorganised and out of control. They were in no position to give orders for they were not focused on planning, directing or controlling.

In this chapter we will look at the role of a supervisor or manager in giving directions and monitoring results.

Giving orders

Employees have two main questions, 'What do you want me to do?' and 'Am I getting it right?'. If a manager gives clear instructions, the second question is answered when the employee sees that things are turning out as required by the manager. This internal feedback is rewarding. External feedback given by the supervisor is also rewarding. However to reach the desired level of performance, the employee first needs to be given very clear instructions. This was covered to some degree in Chapter 6 on training, where the importance of being logical, explaining key steps and giving the reasons for them was discussed, and will be dealt with further in this chapter where the emphasis will be on controlling performance by providing feedback.

To use a simple example, if you asked someone to make a 'good' cup of tea they would be confused about what you meant by 'good'. If, on the other hand, you asked them to make a 'strong' cup of tea they would know exactly what you meant. This may be an over-simplistic example, but many managers expect their staff to provide 'good' service without being clear about what this is. When giving orders, supervisors and managers should consider the following guidelines:

- Be specific about what you expect.
- Be logical in the order of tasks.
- Ensure that your instructions are comprehensive; don't make assumptions.
- Explain why it is important to do things in a particular way.
- Show the person how to do them (especially when it comes to communicating with customers).
- Check for understanding.

Delegation

Delegation occurs when a staff member is given the authority to carry out a task which is normally the responsibility of someone more senior. For example, cashing up and closing at the end of a day's trading is one of the roles a manager may delegate to a supervisor. Likewise, a supervisor may delegate the job of ordering new menus to a more junior employee. In delegating a job to someone else you give them the responsibility for carrying out the task but you still retain accountability. If something should go wrong you are accountable for the result. This of course is the basis for the expression, 'the buck stops here'. When you delegate tasks you enable staff at lower levels to develop their own skills in supervision and to increase their motivation by giving them responsibility. However, when you delegate, you also need to have a system for control, to check to see that everything is going as expected. This means that you need to monitor results on an ongoing basis.

Control

To check to see that tasks are being performed correctly a supervisor needs a system for control. This should cover all tasks, normal duties as well as those tasks delegated to other staff members. Since it is impossible to watch everyone working, a supervisor or manager needs to develop other ways of monitoring staff performance. Reports on stock movements, for example, can tell you whether there are variances or unexpected shortages. These could be due to waste or theft but, in either case, it would be immediately evident that more control was needed over stock movements.

There are three factors that need to be considered when checking on efficiency and service: processes, products and people.

Controlling processes

In the last chapter the importance of sequencing tasks in a particular order was discussed and illustrated. The processes involved were seen to be the keys to success. The same principles would apply in the case of a banquet department where staff might serve several hundred guests at a time, but the process would need to be planned and controlled by careful monitoring. Fig. 8.1 shows how processes can be monitored.

Fig. 8.1

Process for banquet service.

Dinner service

A team of two will serve each table. Each team will be responsible for two tables, that is 16 guests.

A and B set up for service.

A and B stand by to seat guests, one at each table.

A and B provide beverage service, one at each table.

A serves bread to both tables while B continues with beverage service for both tables.

A serves entrée to both tables while B continues with beverage service for both tables.

A and B serve main meals to both tables, one at each table.

The supervisor can tell at a glance which stage of service each table has reached and therefore keep control of the service process.

Controlling products

While service processes are important in the banquet area, they are equally important behind the scenes in the kitchen where hundreds of hot meals are being prepared for simultaneous service. Tasks are allocated and checked to ensure that all processes will come together when the food is plated for service. At this point the banquet chefs check each plate leaving the kitchen to ensure that the product meets exacting standards of presentation.

In the hospitality industry both processes and products are important, whereas in some industries only the end product is important. A plate of food might look very appetising even though it might be full of unpleasant, but invisible, bacteria due to cross-contamination (which can occur in the preparation process). For reasons such as this, the supervisor must focus on both processes and outcomes. Further examples of processes and products that need to be monitored are shown in Table 8.1.

Controlling people

In previous chapters we discussed theories of leadership and motivation. In this chapter we return to these topics to look more specifically at setting performance standards and ensuring that these standards are met. Having established performance standards, it is then a matter of providing feedback to staff, both informally and formally. This answers the question posed by most employees, 'How am I doing?', as mentioned earlier.

Table 8.1

Examples of processes and products.

Processes	Products
using safe lifting techniques	meeting room set-up
recording reservations	confirmation letter
costing new menu items	menu
ordering new linen	room décor/presentation
cashing up	daily report
handling complaints	letter of apology
patrolling and checking premises	checklist

Managing staff performance should involve consultation with employees. Consulting staff on the establishment of procedures and standards of performance will ensure that there are no hidden assumptions and, most importantly, that the standards are achievable. The procedure for opening and serving wine is shown in Table 8.2. As you can see, the procedure outlines the steps in the process and the standard describes the level of performance expected.

If performance is monitored consistently, staff will feel that their treatment is fair and equitable. If, on the other hand, performance is monitored in a haphazard way, staff will feel unsettled and anxious. Performance monitoring should be a positive approach to providing good service by giving guidance and advice.

There is a tendency for supervisors to pay attention only to the poor performers. This leaves those who excel feeling frustrated that their contributions are not acknowledged. Being noticed is important, and this is one of the simplest ways to encourage staff.

In providing positive feedback you need to ensure that the feedback you give is specific. That way it will be more rewarding. When you give feedback it should follow the model, 'When you (did something specific) then (the following positive result occurred)'. To give you an example, if you were giving positive feedback on customer service you might say, 'When you smiled and greeted the

Table 8.2

Standards and procedures in serving wine.

Task	Procedure	Standard of Performance
Wine service	1 Present the bottle to the host before opening.	Hold label towards host. Carry a waiter's cloth.
	2 Confirm the name of the wine ordered. vintage.	Speak clearly. State the name and
	3 Open the wine.	Follow safety guidelines when using wine opener.
	4 Place cork on table next to host.	Hold bottle firmly and remove cork discreetly.
	5 Pour wine for host to taste.	Pour 60 ml. Move clockwise.
	6 Pour all guest glasses and then return to fill host glass.	Pour two-thirds full. Twist bottle to avoid spills. Don't touch glass with bottle.

customer so cheerfully, her face really lit up. I am sure that's why customers keep coming back to you for the friendly service you provide.' Compare this with 'Well done'. As you can see, the specific feedback is more positive and more likely to motivate the employee.

This process is illustrated in Fig. 8.2.

Fig. 8.2

Positive feedback.

When you . . . then. (+ve)

Of course there are situations in which performance needs to be corrected. Once again, the feedback should be specific as should the explanation of what is required to correct the situation. The formula for giving corrective feedback is, 'When you (did something specific) then (the following negative result occurred). If you (were to do something correctly) then (the following positive result would occur).' To give an example, you might say, 'When you don't look up from your work when a customer walks in, she feels that you are not interested in her request. If you look up and smile, she will feel that you are giving your undivided attention and will be impressed with your professional service.' This process is illustrated in Fig. 8.3. Very often supervisors give the first part of this feedback without explaining what is required. If someone doesn't know what 'good' service looks like, telling them to improve their poor customer service skills is a waste of time. The second part, which describes specifically the behaviour you require, is the most useful in coaching staff.

Fig. 8.3

Positive feedback.

When you . . . then (–nve).   If you . . . then (+ve).

In some cases staff have not been trained and you need to provide them with more than a few words of coaching and encouragement. They need to have the whole task shown to them in accordance with the approach described in Chapter 6. Where interpersonal communication or customer service is involved you, the supervisor, need to demonstrate how this should be done. In this way you become a role model, demonstrating best practice so that your staff can copy you.

One of the most frustrating things for staff is being 'blamed' for things outside their control. If there are factors which contribute to their poor performance, such as a computer breakdown or an unexpected delay or accident, these should be acknowledged. Unfortunately, when things go wrong, there is a tendency to blame people and not circumstances. This is known as attribution error. A good supervisor should not attribute poor performance to lack of effort when there are external contributing factors.

As you can see from these guidelines, monitoring people involves keeping close to the action, knowing specifically what you are looking for in good performance and providing your staff with feedback on their performance. This will enable them to develop their full potential. Fig. 8.4 clearly illustrates a problem-solving approach to performance problems.

Appraising performance

Most management of workplace performance occurs informally by supervisors giving instructions and advice, and providing feedback on the spot. When, for example, a supervisor adjusts a table setting it is a form of feedback — without a word the staff member is shown that the setting has not met the supervisor's exacting standards. Most positive feedback is given informally, too — a smile, a pat on the back, a friendly nod, all indicate that things are going well.

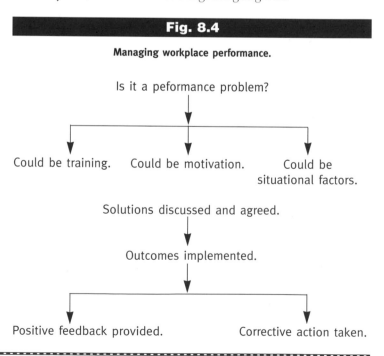

Fig. 8.4

Managing workplace performance.

Is it a peformance problem?

Could be training.   Could be motivation.   Could be situational factors.

Solutions discussed and agreed.

Outcomes implemented.

Positive feedback provided.   Corrective action taken.

In addition to this informal feedback which takes place on a day-to-day basis, some establishments have a formal performance appraisal system. This involves an interview during which the manager and staff member look at the past and the future. In looking at the past, performance is appraised and in many cases it is ranked on a performance scale. In looking at the future, the two participants analyse training needs and career plans to come up with performance objectives and plans for their achievement. This interview provides a rare opportunity for some quality time to be spent on the questions, 'What do you expect?' and 'How am I doing?', and the question, 'Where am I going?' is also addressed.

Many performance appraisal forms are based on general performance criteria such as efficiency, reliability, teamwork and customer relations. Unfortunately some of these criteria are so general that they are difficult to use in providing performance feedback, simply because they are not always closely related to the specific requirements of the job. Looking back at the job description in Fig. 5.3 in Chapter 5, it would be possible to take the duties listed and use these instead to create a form which could be used in a performance appraisal interview. This would be likely to generate productive discussion about workplace performance, training needs and the hurdles that prevent effective performance. A two-way discussion allows for problem-solving as well as for recognition and reward for meeting performance standards. A performance appraisal form developed in conjunction with the above job description is illustrated in Fig. 8.5 on the following page.

As you can see, a form devised using a job description enables the supervisor to discuss performance which is directly relevant to the job. Performance objectives and training plans would likewise relate closely to the job's requirements.

In planning and conducting the performance appraisal interview you should:

- advise the employee beforehand of the aim of the performance appraisal session
- organise a time and place free from interruption
- create an appropriate climate for the interview
- review specific job performance against specific job targets
- give performance feedback
- openly discuss issues which have an impact on performance
- agree on new performance targets

Fig. 8.5

Appraisal form developed using a job description as a guide.

Performance Appraisal Report

Position Title: Housekeeping Attendant	**Name:**
Reports to: Housekeeping Supervisor	**Name:**

Duties

Pick up daily report for rooms allocated, sign out keys and check with supervisor for priorities.

Comment:

Prepare housekeeping trolley with supplies and linen.
Comment:

Clean rooms according to hotel specifications.
Comment:

Report maintenance defects.
Comment:

Complete room reports and notify housekeeping supervisor immediately after cleaning.
Comment:

Greet guests and provide information where requested.
Comment:

Log lost property with supervisor.
Comment:

Observe Occupational Health and Safety guidelines.
Comment:

Report suspicious and other incidents to security.
Comment:

Carry out other duties as requested.
Comment:

Job Summary

Responsible for room cleaning, replenishment of guest supplies, reporting problems to maintenance or security and customer relations. Key roles are maintaining high standards of cleanliness and presentation and providing quality customer service. Thirteen to 14 rooms per day, 30 minutes per room, plus other cleaning duties as allocated

Performance rating:

poor	below average	average	above average	excellent
[ ]	[ ]	[ ]	[ ]	[ ]

General comments on overall performance:

Agreed performance objectives and timelines:

Career development plans:

Signature:
Supervisor

Signature:
Staff member:

- agree on steps to be taken to achieve these targets
- agree on timelines for achievement of targets
- ask employee to sum up the discussion
- end on a positive note
- follow up on the interview.

Managing discipline issues

In any disciplinary situation, the employee should be able to say that performance expectations were clear. If the recommendations of this book have been followed this should be the case. Disciplinary problems can be prevented by developing job descriptions and induction and training plans, and by providing ongoing advice. If, however, this informal feedback does not resolve a performance problem, more definite corrective action needs to be taken. This disciplinary process involves three steps.

Verbal warning

The first step is to document the discussion in which you give the employee corrective feedback. This can be recorded in a diary or a log book. During the discussion the employee should be told:

- what behaviour is unacceptable
- why it is unacceptable
- what needs to be done to remedy the situation (specifically)
- what positive result this will produce.
- that failure to comply with the request will lead to a written warning
- a date for review of the situation.

If, for example, an employee were continually arriving late for work, the verbal warning (and subsequent written warnings) should follow the above format. Following is an example:

Zack, you have arrived late for work three times this week and this has meant that we were not ready for service when the first customers arrived. Please make sure that you get to work 10 minutes before your shift so that you have time to change into your uniform. If you start on time the mise-en-place will be ready and service will flow smoothly. If this does not improve it could lead to a written warning. I feel confident that you will be able to organise your time to arrive 10 minutes before your shift and will discuss this with you at the same time next week.

Written warning

This time the warning is in writing. Again it should state the problem and the solution and give a deadline for its resolution. The employee should be warned that failure to meet the prescribed performance standards could lead to dismissal. This letter should be witnessed and kept on the employee's file.

Final written warning

The final warning letter should state what needs to be done, making it clear that failure to comply with the directions given will lead to dismissal.

SUMMARY

Performance management has been covered in this chapter, in particular monitoring and control. The importance of establishing clear expectations and agreeing on performance standards so that both supervisor and staff know where they stand has been emphasised. New staff members should be given a job description, provided with appropriate training and given specific feedback on job-related performance. Supervisors are not only responsible for monitoring and controlling people, but also processes and products. In the course of their duties, they sometimes need to delegate some of their responsibilities but, as it has been pointed out, they still remain accountable for the results. Well-trained and well-motivated staff make the supervisor's role easier as they are keen to take on additional roles, they perform successfully and they achieve the targets of the work team.

Of course this three-step process would not apply to situations in which serious misconduct occurred. In situations such as being drunk on duty the employee would be asked to leave immediately.

While some managers become anxious about the disciplinary process, there are others who are very clear about their expectations and let their staff know exactly where they stand. One such department has the lowest staff turnover in the industry and the highest levels of staff motivation. Although unsatisfactory performance can lead to a warning from the department manager, good performance is routinely encouraged. This department has a strong emphasis on coaching staff, providing positive feedback and team building. As a result, staff know exactly where they stand and feel positive and confident that they can achieve the department's goals.

Discussion questions

1 What, in your opinion, are some of the tasks that a supervisor cannot delegate? Explain why.
2 What are some personal factors that can affect an employee's workplace performance? To what extent does a supervisor need to take these into account?
3 The word 'specific' is often used in relation to performance feedback. Explain how you would give specific feedback and coaching to someone who was 'rude' to customers.
4 Explain some of the strategies that can prevent workplace performance problems occurring.
5 How would you develop a plan for delegating and controlling the task of managing workplace health and safety?

Case study

Shiela is one of your longest serving employees. She has been with you for six years and has trained all the current staff. Lately she has had a number of serious family problems and has been unwell, taking numerous sick days.

Plan a quiet discussion with her to reach a win-win solution to this problem. In readiness for the interview with her:

- Prepare a record of her absences from work.
- List reasons why this is a burden for you and the other staff.
- Develop some open questions for exploring the issues.
- Prepare comments on her long and reliable service prior to this problem occurring.
- Decide how far your role extends to being a professional personal counsellor.
- Develop a range of possible compromises for a win-win solution.
- Write to her at home (she has been off work for two weeks) explaining what you would like to achieve in the interview.

CHAPTER NINE

decision-making and
problem-solving

On completion of this chapter you will be able to:

- explain the importance of decision-making and problem-solving
- outline a range of situations in which decision-making and problem-solving are required (operational and customer service perspectives)
- develop a problem-solving strategy
- apply a problem-solving strategy
- evaluate problem-solving strategies for their short and long-term effectiveness.

THE CHEF WAS FOOLING AROUND IN THE KITCHEN WITH A HELIUM balloon left over from the wedding the night before. The balloon floated up to the neon light, it exploded and the tube shattered into a thousand pieces. Several people received small cuts and the shock of the exploding glass left them very shaken. There was glass in everything. We had to close the restaurant immediately because there was glass in the food, in the cooking oil, and in all the cooking equipment. It took two days before we could open again. The supervisor on duty made the decision to close immediately and personally apologised to all the customers and escorted them to the door. Then she came into the kitchen, made everyone stop trying to clean up, checked on all the injuries to make sure they weren't serious and talked through the whole thing with us. She calmed everyone down. A couple of people were shaking from the shock. None of us knew what to do. She took some extra time with the chef because he was feeling worst of all. Months later we were able to laugh about it, and we became quite a close team having survived the experience together. When I asked her if she had nightmares about it she said that she only had nightmares about the restaurant losing money!

This case study illustrates the type of 'one-off' problems that can occur in the tourism and hospitality industry. These are termed non-recurrent problems. Other problems are recurrent because they happen over and over again. For instance, a shortage of skilled staff is often a recurring problem, especially with large events where the establishment is reliant on casual staff.

Table 9.1

Examples of recurrent and non-recurrent problems.

Recurrent Problems — Examples	Non-recurrent Problems — Examples
shortages in supplies	fire
equipment breakdowns	hold-up
shortages of staff	interpersonal conflict
computer failure	theft
cancellations	union action
late arrivals	customer complaints
overbooking	legal action

Examples of both recurrent and non-recurrent problems are listed in Table 9.1.

Turning problems into opportunities

Decision-making is the process of choosing a course of action. Some decisions are fairly simple, such as selecting a new casual employee or purchasing new equipment. Neither of these situations is a problem situation. Problem-solving involves decision-making but it generally requires more analysis, a broader and more complex range of solutions and, finally, a decision on the best course of action. The word 'problem' implies difficulty and one hotel chain banned the word and called every problem an 'opportunity'. They felt that a problem is an opportunity to seek a creative solution to a complex issue and preferred the positive emphasis of 'opportunity'.

Any organisation that embraces problems and learns from them is a learning organisation. Continuous improvement is the basis for quality improvement and, for this to occur, problems need to be tackled head on. Learning organisations encourage feedback from customers, even insisting that their staff ask for feedback, and view both positive and negative feedback as opportunities to improve the way they operate. Unfortunately many businesses don't encourage this, and in fact staff are too frightened to tell their supervisors about problems.

The hospitality industry is one of the most challenging of all industries for five reasons:

• Many of the products sold are perishable (you can't use a limp lettuce).

- You are satisfying primary needs such as hunger, thirst and tiredness.
- All of your business tends to happen in a rush.
- Customer accounts are opening and closing in a very short time (not 30 days).
- The level of trade is often hard to predict.

Because of these challenges, the hospitality workplace experiences problems all the time. On a quiet Wednesday 25 people might turn up for lunch and all order the same dish, or several guests may ask to extend their stay when the hotel is absolutely full. One of the biggest challenges for a particular function centre occurred when a large group at an outdoor wedding in a nearby park decided to find a new venue when it started to rain! They all walked in and asked if a function could be set up on the spot!

Problem-solving is therefore the core business of the hospitality industry.

In the travel sector, the main role of the travel agent is to solve problems. In many cases the problem is finding the cheapest fare and accommodation at the highest possible value for money. This involves exploring a considerable number of options and relies on the travel agent's knowledge of destinations and products, their ability to use high level technical and computing skills and to access up-to-date information on current packages, and their patience with customers who often change their minds many times!

Stages in problem-solving

We will use a case study to illustrate the stages it is necessary to go through to solve problems. These stages are also illustrated in Fig. 9.1.

Define the problem

The first thing to do is to define the problem. This analysis often solves the problem immediately, in the best cases leading you to decide that it is not your problem or that there is absolutely nothing that can be done about it.

In our example you are a supervisor in the catering outlet of a busy airport. One of your staff has not turned up for breakfast service. The cafeteria opens at 6.30 am and the first staff member arrives at 5.30 am to set up for the day. The cashier should arrive at 6.30 am together with another server to manage the busy breakfast rush. On this

Fig. 9.1

Stages in problem-solving.

Define the problem

↓

Analyse the problem

↓

Develop a range of solutions

↓

Test the solutions

↓

Decide on the best solution

↓

Take action

↓

Follow through

occasion you arrive at 6.45 am to find that the cashier has not turned up for work and that there are delayed airline departures this morning. This means that you and your staff will be under extreme pressure.

Analyse the problem

The next stage in the problem-solving process is to analyse the extent and severity of the problem. This often helps to clarify your thinking and is a precursor to the next stage, which is developing possible solutions.

The difficulty you are experiencing in your cafeteria is that you don't know whether this person is late or not coming at all. None of the other staff is trained to use the register. Your usual duties include fetching supplies from the main store, fetching change for the register, and supervising and assisting. If you take over the register, you will not have time to get enough supplies of food items, such as pastries and soft drinks, to last the morning. Service will also be slow and queues will develop. You can count on it that the airport manager will notice!

Develop a range of solutions

It is useful to develop a range of solutions as you usually come up with some solutions to the problem that are easier to implement than others. In this case, one of the options is to try to find out what has happened to your cashier. Another option is to try to find a replacement. The third option is for you to operate the register, despite the shortage of products that will inevitably occur later in the morning.

Test the solutions

Solutions can be tested for their short-term and long-term implications. In this case there is no time to follow the first two options since queues will develop while you are on the phone in your office. Although some products will not be available later in the morning, you feel sure that customers would rather be served quickly even though some of their choices may not be available.

Decide on the best solution

The next stage is to decide on the best solution. In this case, you decide that the best option is to ensure that customers are not kept waiting even though you are aware that there may be complaints later on. You can also remain hopeful that the cashier will turn up or that help will become available from another section.

Take action

Taking action to solve a problem is the most important stage. In many cases of conflict in the workplace, supervisors find the situation so complex and threatening that they take no action at all. In the case of the cashier who was late, feedback will have to be given, and perhaps a warning if this is not the first occurrence.

Follow through

The final stage in problem-solving involves following through. In cases where customers have been dissatisfied and have complained, this is a most important process, and one which can turn a customer into a loyal supporter! In the example provided for discussion, the supervisor might reflect on the fact that there was too much reliance on one person's skills and think about training one of the other servers to use the register. He might also realise (too late) that he had not solved one aspect of the problem, which was having enough change for the cash register!

Table 9.2

Variables in the decision-making process.

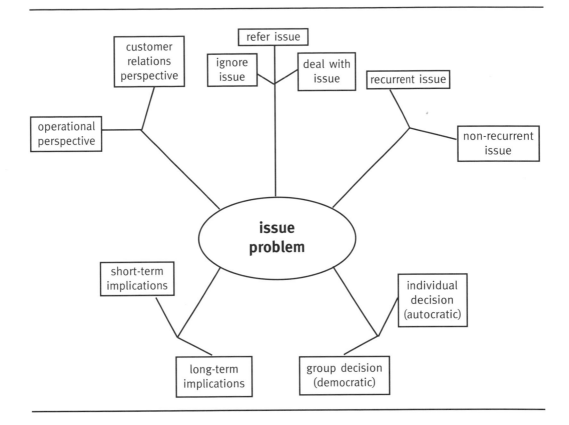

Variables in decision-making and problem-solving

When making decisions and solving problems supervisors must take into account a wide range of factors (variables). Competent leaders look at issues from various perspectives, analyse short and long-term implications and consider the importance of involving other people in the decision-making process. A range of these variables are shown in Fig. 9.2.

Importance of the issue

Some issues can be safely ignored. Some need to be referred to senior management for their consideration. An industrial relations issue, for example, would need to be discussed with senior management and human resources staff. Others can be dealt with directly because they are within the scope of the supervisory or management role.

Recurrent or non-recurrent issue?

Recurrent problems occur over and over and for this reason they need to be solved. If the fax machine regularly runs out of paper and supplies are not available this will have an impact on day-to-day operations and increase the frustration of both staff and clients. Non-recurrent problems are 'one off' situations, and very often decisions can be made quickly, providing that the issue is not too important or too dangerous. An emergency situation is an example of an important but non-recurrent problem. Because the decision has such serious implications, it needs to be reviewed and analysed to ensure that future critical incidents are dealt with in the best possible way. One such incident is outlined in the case study at the end of the chapter.

Operational and customer relations perspectives

Issues often need to be looked at from both an operational and a customer relations perspective. If, for example, a customer is particularly demanding, asking for a dish which is complex and time consuming to prepare (especially if a kitchen assistant needs to be sent to a nearby restaurant to borrow ingredients!), both operational and customer relations perspectives need to be considered. If the level of business is low, this customer's request can be met. However, if the kitchen is busy, this will be out of the question from an operational point of view.

Individual and group perspectives

Many decisions have implications for team members and therefore their involvement in reaching the decision is essential. There is a range of benefits of group decision-making, including creative synergy, the presence of different decision-making styles, the advantages of brainstorming, high levels of participation and support, and high levels of motivation. On the other hand, group decision-making processes can be time consuming. A phenomenon called 'social loafing' can also occur where the combined effort of the group is less than the effort that would be made by individuals operating independently.

Long and short-term implications

Finally the long and short-term implications of the decision need to be considered. Sometimes short-term solutions create long-term problems. For example, a manager might call the police in response to an accusation that a staff member's money has been stolen. This would create a high level of anxiety in the office and the damage done to the group might be permanent even if the staff member 'remembered' later where he had spent it!

Discussion questions

1 Discuss the pros and cons of group decision-making.
2 Give examples of situations in which individual (or autocratic) decisions need to be made by a manager.
3 In response to complaints about meals from hospital patients, a catering supervisor decides to brainstorm the issues with catering staff and nurses. Discuss whether this is the most appropriate response to these complaints and why.
4 A customer complains about a meal in the pub after eating it all! How would you respond to this situation?
5 Responsible service of alcohol is one of the most difficult situations requiring decision-making by management. Develop guidelines for a new supervisor on situations where alcohol should be refused.

Case studies

In your role as supervisor you encounter two types of problems in relation to workplace health, safety and security. Some of these problems are recurrent problems (they happen again and again) and others are non-recurrent. You need to look at both types of problems. Some are minor problems and others have serious implications.

Problem One (recurrent)

Your staff are not wearing correct uniforms in the kitchen and this has resulted in accidents which could have been prevented. These accidents include several burns on the arms of staff and one incident where a knife was dropped on the chef's foot. The problem is recurrent because the staff are not complying with uniform regulations which include an approved chef's uniform and safety boots. These workplace accidents reflect a haphazard response to

SUMMARY

In this chapter we have discussed one of the supervisor's or manager's most difficult roles — decision-making and problem-solving. In fact, the distinction between staff member and supervisor rests fundamentally on this decision-making role. Although many day-to-day decisions are made rapidly, numerous variables being considered without realising it, in more complex situations there are great benefits in adopting a systematic approach. This careful reflection on the importance of the decision, its implications and possible outcomes allows leaders to learn from their experience. When colleagues, customers and team members are involved in the decision-making process, support for the decision and win-win solutions are generally achieved.

compliance with workplace performance standards and have led to increases in workers' compensation premiums.

Problem Two (non-recurrent)

A serious fire in the chimney of the pizza oven led to the evacuation of customers, calling of the fire brigade, closure of the establishment for two days, extensive costs for cleaning and repainting, and bad publicity in the local press. This problem is a non-recurrent, one-off incident — or so one hopes!

As supervisor, you are expected to do the following for each of the problems:

- Identify the causes of the problem.
- Explain the leadership approach you would have taken when the problems occurred.
- Plan for discussions with staff with the aim of solving the problems and developing team spirit.
- Develop preventative or contingency plans, including objectives, timelines and delegation of tasks.
- Decide on ways in which staff can be motivated to follow the resultant guidelines or procedures.
- Design a control system or checklist to evaluate progress in achieving the objectives.

CHAPTER TEN

staff
administration

PAPA'S HAD BEEN A FAMILY RESTAURANT FOR 45 YEARS. THE restaurant had been started by Gino in the early 1950s. He and his wife, Maria, had established a solid clientele and over the years had received numerous good reviews in the local papers. As the children grew up they all worked in the restaurant in their spare time. When Gino died, his customers were concerned that the restaurant would close. However, two of the boys decided that they would run the business in their spare time. Tony was a college student in the final stage of a management diploma. His brother, Peter, was three years older and the owner of a gourmet delicatessen. Maria, although close to retirement, still came in to supervise the kitchen and ensure that her famous recipes were being followed to the letter. Four other staff were employed in the restaurant on a permanent part-time basis. After the first few months of operation, things were not going as smoothly as the brothers had hoped. With so little time to spare, they decided to appoint a restaurant manager to oversee the operation. They selected Margaret, who had successfully run her own restaurant before having children and finishing her degree. She was now ready to return to full-time work. Numerous problems occurred, most of which involved communication. Margaret threatened to resign because she said that her position was untenable. She had three bosses giving her conflicting instructions: Tony, Peter and, of course, their mother, Maria. She had understood that she would be running the restaurant and making most of the decisions.

On completion of this chapter you will be able to:

- list the various sectors found within the tourism and hospitality industry
- identify the essential components of an organisational chart
- explain the uses of organisational charts
- describe current changes in relation to organisational planning
- compile an organisational chart
- explain human resource functions
- describe the requirements for staff administration.

This case study illustrates the importance of developing an organisational structure, even where the business is very small. In any business it should be clear who reports to whom. Development of policies and standard methods is another way of ensuring that a business will run smoothly and consistently. Records, including staff records, are an important part of administration.

In this chapter we will look at the structure of the tourism and hospitality industry as well as the structure of hospitality operations.

Tourism and hospitality organisations

The Australian Standard Industry Classification (ASIC) provides a useful overview of the tourism and hospitality industry. Under this system the tourism industry is divided into three major categories which helps to illustrate the difference between 'tourism organisations' and 'hospitality organisations'. This is illustrated in Table 10.1.

This table illustrates the various sectors within the tourism industry. Clearly, however, some organisations in the category, 'restaurants, hotels and clubs', provide products and services to a predominantly local market. The hospitality industry thus meets the needs of both tourists (domestic and international) and local

Table 10.1

Tourism industry structure.

ASIC Major Category	Subdivision	Comment
Wholesale and retail trade	Retail trade	Includes retail shopping such as souvenir shops
Transport and storage	Road transport	Coach, bus, taxi and other
	Rail transport	
	Air transport	Domestic and international air transport
	Services to transport	Includes museums and art galleries, travel agents
Recreation, personal and other services	Entertainment and recreational services	Includes parks and zoos as well as gambling services
	Restaurants, hotels and clubs	All accommodation and food and beverage

How Tourism Labour Markets Work, Research Paper No. 1, Commonwealth Department of Tourism, 1995. © Australian Government Printing Service. Reproduced with permission.

residents. The restaurant described in the case study above would fit into the third major category as it would attract mainly local customers and only a few tourists from other states or overseas.

There are also close relationships between the different tourism sectors, with hotels working closely with travel agents, and retail outlets such as souvenir shops providing services to guests who are accommodated in hotels, motels and guest houses.

Organisational charts

Within a hospitality enterprise an organisational chart is designed to establish the specific relationships between departments and departmental positions. The objective is to give a graphic overview of the lines of authority and the channels of communication. An organisational chart would have been most helpful for the staff working at Papa's as everyone was unsure about their reporting relationships.

Authority should flow in an unbroken line. Line positions are those which make up the chain of command. The role of the supervisor is to be **responsible to** the next level of management and to be **responsible for** his or her work group, as specified in the establishment's organisational chart.

The organisational chart assists in designating responsibilities based on organisational goals. Once responsibilities have been designated to departments and departmental positions they are easier to monitor and control. Organisational charts are also a beneficial training tool in the induction of new employees.

Constructing an organisational chart

It is not difficult to construct an organisational chart once the structure of the business has been determined by management. General rules to follow are:

- Departments and functions should be arranged horizontally with the position titles in boxes of the same size.

Coffee Shop Manager	Bar Manager	Restaurant Manager

- Personnel should be arranged vertically, in accordance with their position or grade.

- All personnel with the same authority level should be on the same horizontal line.

- Unbroken vertical lines are used to show the flow of authority.

- Broken horizontal or vertical lines may be used to show the source of advice and service.

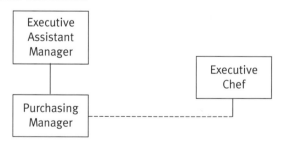

In all organisations an employee should report to only one person. This is called unity of command. In the earlier case study there was considerable confusion about reporting relationships, with the manager of Papa's, the mother and the two brothers giving instructions to staff.

In some cases, however, a person may have more than one reporting relationship. When there is a dual reporting relationship, one of the reporting lines is drawn as a solid line and the other as a dotted line. In a large hotel, for example, the main reporting relationship for a purchasing manager would generally be to the executive assistant manager, with a service relationship to the executive chef, which would be illustrated by a dotted line. This second line is a line of communication rather than a line of authority. However it indicates the importance of service provided to the kitchen by the purchasing department.

In recent times, organisational charts have become flatter, with more responsibility being delegated to lower level staff through the development of self-managed work teams, which has meant that there are now fewer layers of supervision and management. This has occurred mainly in industries where there is a very stable workforce. However, hospitality organisations are increasingly giving more responsibility to frontline staff for on-the-spot decisions in order to enhance customer satisfaction. This has meant that the supervisor is now called less frequently and it has also had implications for training, especially with respect to decision-making.

Examples of organisational charts for small and medium-sized hospitality establishments are illustrated in Figs 10.1 and 10.2.

Fig. 10.1

Organisational chart for a small-sized establishment (motel).

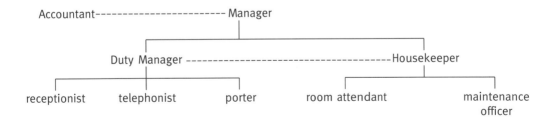

Using an organisational chart

Organisational charts are useful for a number of reasons, as discussed below.

Establishing reporting relationships

Authority is delegated down the organisational chart from the most senior personnel. The expression, 'the buck stops here', refers to the

Fig. 10.2

Organisational chart for a medium-sized hospitality establishment.

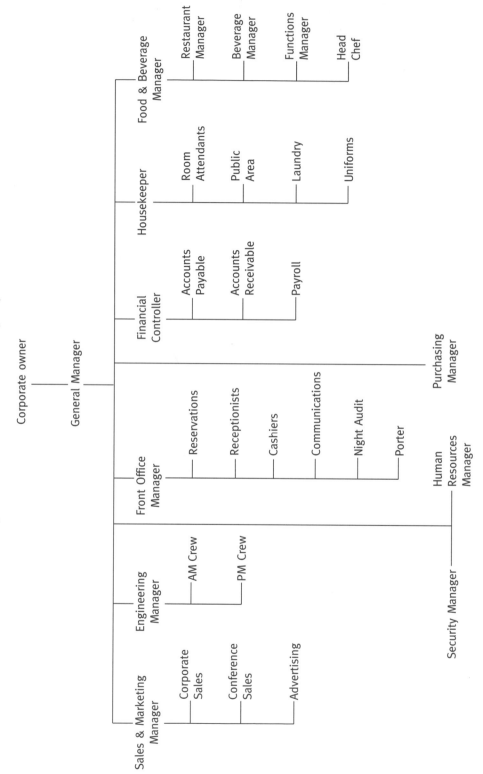

Fig. 10.3

Two different types of organisational chart.

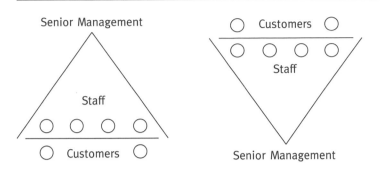

person who holds the role at the top of the organisational hierarchy. However, some organisations draw their organisational charts upside down, with the customer at the top (see Fig. 10.3). This non-traditional approach emphasises the value of the customer to the organisation.

Establishing communication channels

The lines drawn on an organisational chart show the formal channels of communication. If an employee wishes to make a suggestion or voice a complaint, the very first step is to talk to the person at the next level on the chart. This is generally a supervisor or assistant manager.

Monitoring and controlling activities

By defining responsibilities for various levels in the hierarchy it is much easier to monitor activities and implement control measures. For example, it may be the supervisor's responsibility to maintain stocks of cutlery in the restaurant. Although the supervisor may delegate the responsibility for this task to one of her staff, she is ultimately responsible for maintaining stock levels. The organisational chart is thus an important part of the planning process.

Training staff

When training staff, the organisational chart is a very useful tool for describing the various departments and roles within the organisation and the relationships between the different departments or sections.

Administering staff

Human resource management records

The objective of maintaining human resource records is to assist management in performing the necessary human resource functions. Supervisors are generally involved in the implementation of human resource policies and play an active role in many of the human resource functions. For example, they often conduct employee performance appraisals in accordance with a format provided by the human resources department. In smaller operations, the manager usually plans as well as implements human resource functions.

Human resource functions

The following are the major human resource functions:

- forecasting future staffing needs in accordance with anticipated requirements
- negotiating and liaising with unions
- ensuring the health, safety and welfare of employees
- developing and implementing training for new recruits and existing employees
- formulating policy in regard to terms and conditions of employment
- ensuring compliance with relevant employment legislation
- managing and reviewing wages, salary packages and staff superannuation.

Maintaining legal records

Under Federal and State statutes and awards, employers are legally obligated to keep records about specific human resource matters. The requirements vary from State to State, depending on the relevant legislation. Employers should consult relevant awards to determine their obligations and pass on administration of the requirements of those awards to the appropriate managers or supervisors.

Keeping records on individual employees

Individual employee records contain confidential information so access to these files must be strictly controlled. However, individual employees should be allowed access to information kept on file about themselves.

Fig. 10.4

Sample staff record card.

Staff Record

Personal Details

Second Name _____ First Name _____ Title _____

Address _____

Telephone _____

Emergency Contact _____ Work Visa Status _____

Position Details

Position Title _____ Department _____

Commencement Date _____ Status (part-time, full-time)

Salary/Wage $ _____ Allowances $ _____

Last Day Worked_____

Resignation ☐   Dismissal ☐   Rehire? Yes/No ☐

Comment (note warnings)

_____

_____

_____

_____

_____

_____

Banking

Bank _____ Branch _____ Account No. _____

Approvals

Position Change ☐   Salary/Wage ☐   Status ☐

Recommended _____

Authorised _____

Actioned _____

Date _____

The following records should be kept in an employee's file. These records assist in the human resource function of ensuring fair and equal treatment of all employees.

1 Application form

2 Pre-employment interview records

3 Wage, salary and superannuation records

4 Study and training records

5 Career development since joining the organisation

6 Performance appraisals and counselling records

7 Grievance records

8 Absence, lateness, accident and medical records

9 Disciplinary records, including warnings and suspensions

10 Termination and final interview records.

SUMMARY

In this chapter we have delineated the various sectors of the tourism industry and have indicated how these overlap with sectors of the hospitality industry. We have looked at how organisational charts are used by tourism and hospitality organisations, large and small, to assist in planning, allocation of responsibilities, clarification of reporting relationships and the control process. Administration of staff has also been covered, with an emphasis on the necessity for keeping accurate employee records.

Staff records also assist in the compilation of statistical information that management can use to plan for the future, for example the number of people applying for positions, average levels of pay, absenteeism and labour turnover.

It is vital that any documentation relating to human resources is completed accurately and promptly in order to safeguard against any insurance, industrial relations, legal or other issues that may arise. Copies of documentation must be filed for easy access and distributed to the relevant department heads and union officials.

A sample staff record card is shown in Fig. 10.4 on the previous page, although most staff records are now stored in computer systems.

Discussion questions

1 *Why is it better for employees to report to one person only?*

2 *The structure and design of organisational charts has changed over recent years. What are these changes and what factors have influenced them?*

3 *How does the inclusion of an organisational chart in a training manual benefit a new employee?*

4 *What do some designers of organisational charts do when the chart gets too wide on the lower levels (see Fig. 10.2)?*

5 *As a supervisor it is your responsibility to monitor and control your employees' behaviour to ensure compliance with in-house*

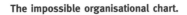

Fig. 10.5

The impossible organisational chart.

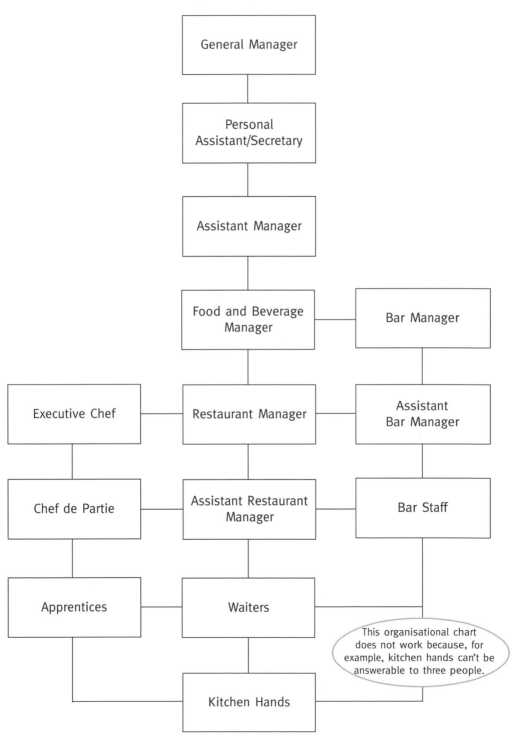

policies. What documentation would you complete and to whom would you distribute the information in the following situations?

- *A staff member served a patron who was obviously drunk. A formal complaint was filed by another patron who was injured when the drunk patron fell and knocked her over. A verbal warning was given about responsible service of alcohol.*
- *A new staff member has taken a sick day for the last three Sundays in a row.*
- *A formal complaint has been made to you regarding the sexual harassment of an employee by another staff member.*

Case study

An organisational chart which needs correction has been provided in Fig. 10.5 on page 119. First improve the chart, then develop an organisational chart for Papa's, the restaurant described at the beginning of the chapter.

CHAPTER ELEVEN

staff
scheduling

I have worked as a supervisor in all sorts of tourism establishments. Some have had very stable casual staff (especially those in small towns) while others have had an incredibly high turnover of casuals. Although you need to be able to respond to highs and lows in the level of business — and casual staff allow you to do this — you also need to provide some stability for the other employees or they will leave. In the smaller places I noticed that although the hours changed for the casual staff they were more or less guaranteed a minimum number of hours a month. If they could not be given the hours, they were told of this well in advance. It is a tricky balancing act. In the big cities this balance doesn't seem to exist. In banquet departments, for example, you often have a different crew for nearly every function. This makes training and supervision very difficult.

In the best places I have worked, the casual staff have been used to manage the peaks and lows, but at the same time there has been careful consideration of their needs and the investment that has been put into their training. In my view, you need to have the right mix of permanent staff working flexible hours, with a few casuals rostered on for the busy periods.

W e are largely dependent upon a casual labour market in the tourism industry, and with good reason. Our industry, like many others, experiences peak periods and low periods of business, particularly if catering for a particular market segment. For example, hotels geared towards corporate clients tend to be quieter during school holiday periods. Resorts located in a

On completion of this chapter you will be able to:

- **assess levels of business**
- **develop staffing plans to cope with levels of business**
- **check awards and agreements for issues relating to staff scheduling**
- **discuss costs associated with staffing**
- **organise the best staffing mix for cost-effective use of labour**
- **allocate duties to ensure the most appropriate skills mix and the most effective use of staff**
- **take employee needs into account in staff scheduling**
- **maintain staff records.**

seasonal environment, such as the ski resorts of southern Australia, need to have flexibility of employment conditions. While a casual labour market allows flexibility in rostering hours, it may not be as cost effective as it seems due to inconsistency in standards of service and higher staff turnover.

The conditions and allowances applicable to the terms of full-time, part-time and casual employment vary and need to be understood by the supervisor. Wages costs are calculated as a percentage of sales revenue, and budgets are set by the financial controller or the owner of the business. It is the supervisor's responsibility to maintain or improve on budgetary projections.

Effects of awards and agreements

Award conditions may affect staff scheduling and labour costs. As awards vary from State to State and are regulated by the sector of the industry in which you are working, it is difficult to be specific. Some awards cover several States, while others apply to only one State or Territory. The Department of Industrial Relations can be consulted regarding the appropriate award for a business or occupational classification. Awards cover pay rates, meal breaks, hours of work and other conditions of employment.

Examples of awards include the following:

- Accommodation, Hotels, Resorts and Gaming Award (Victoria, New South Wales, Tasmania, South East Queensland)
- Motels, Accommodation and Resorts Award (Victoria, New South Wales, Tasmania, South East Queensland)
- Liquor Trades Hotels Award (Australian Capital Territory)
- Hotels, Motels, Wine Saloons, Catering, Accommodation, Clubs and Casinos Award (Northern Territory)
- Cafe Restaurant and Catering Award (Queensland)

Some workplaces have their own agreements. These agreements are negotiated locally, generally with staff in a single organisation. Sheraton Hotels and Hamilton Island Resort, for example, have negotiated their own agreements with staff.

You will need to investigate the awards or agreements that affect your work situation. Some factors arising from awards or agreements that may affect scheduling and labour costs are:

- the hours of work agreed upon or set by the relevant award for full-time, part-time and casual employees

- the spread of hours
- minimum breaks between shifts
- wage rates (including minimum wages)
- sickness pay
- overtime rates
- annual leave
- allowances (uniform, tool, meal, etc.)
- apprenticeship award conditions
- traineeship award conditions
- public holidays
- board and lodgings
- long service leave
- maternity/adoption leave
- accident pay
- days off coinciding with public holidays
- bereavement leave
- superannuation.

Scheduling and staffing costs are governed by two concerns: the time it takes to perform the task and the rates of pay for the employees scheduled.

With a function, such as a wedding or a convention, staff would be required to set up the furniture, set tables and bar areas, prepare food in the kitchen, serve food and drinks, disassemble on completion of the function, wash, polish and store all crockery, glassware and cutlery, and leave the kitchen spotlessly clean.

Awards (or agreements) state that employees are entitled to have a meal break after a certain number of hours, so often supervisors will stagger the start and finish times of a function to stay within the limit of hours outlined in the award, thus eliminating meal allowances and overtime penalties. An employee should be scheduled when their skills are able to be maximised, for example a casual chef might be scheduled for the peak periods of service only as they are on a higher hourly rate than, say, an apprentice, who can do a lot of the preparation, and/or a steward who can clean the kitchen at the end of the shift.

Scheduling needs to be designed around your peak and low periods of business. An efficient supervisor records and utilises historical data to assist in forecasting business patterns. To be overstaffed is not cost effective; to be understaffed causes customer complaints and staff dissatisfaction. Achieving the correct balance is one of the most difficult tasks facing frontline managers.

Assessing levels of business

The following statistical reports can be used to predict demand which will, in turn, assist you with scheduling staff.

Sales records

These show the level of business for previous days, weeks or years. For example, the level of business on the previous Valentine's Day or Father's Day, and the number of staff scheduled, would help in preparing staff rosters for those days in the current year.

Hourly tallies

Hourly tallies assist in predicting the peaks and lows within the daily hours of trading. For example, a supervisor of a bottle shop might tally the number of sales for particular periods of the day by reading the information from the point-of-sale terminal. If the information were then plotted on a bar chart or run chart it would be easy to view peak and low periods. Simultaneously, peak delivery periods of supplies and associated tasks could be plotted on another chart. This combination of data would ensure that staff, particularly casual staff, were scheduled in accordance with productivity requirements.

Daily tallies

These are useful in determining the busier and quieter days of the week and in scheduling rostered days off for permanent and part-time staff. Supervisors review the cash register tapes or dockets, or analyse the reports generated by point-of-sale terminals, and record the number of covers at the close of trading. The sales mix of the day — the number of entrees, mains, desserts and beverages sold — is often reviewed as well.

Occupancy reports

Establishments offering accommodation check the daily occupancy rates for the forthcoming weeks and base scheduling for the housekeeping department and front office on the number of expected in-house guests. Other revenue-producing departments, such as restaurants and bars, will also be affected by the number of in-house guests and will need to schedule accordingly. Of particular concern are large groups of people, such as convention delegates, staying at the establishment as they tend to dine together.

Communication between departments regarding the movements and requirements of groups is imperative.

The average hotel or motel occupancy rate over a month is generally plotted on a yearly planner, allowing a comparison of peak periods and low periods over several years which assists in scheduling refurbishment of rooms and planning annual leave periods for staff. Similarly, an analysis of peak and low trading periods in a restaurant provides useful data for staff scheduling. The sales report illustrated in Fig. 11.1 on pages 126–27 shows that the Crab Claw Restaurant is very busy on Fridays and Saturdays, with over 300 covers, while the early part of the week is very slow, with only 65 covers on Monday.

Accurate forecasting is dependent upon a constant review of what was planned and what actually happened on the day. If wages costs exceed the budgeted amount, management needs to know why. To assist in this procedure, wages for additional staff members rostered on at the last minute and any overtime must be recorded. If the period of business was unusually slow or unusually busy, this information should also be recorded.

Ensuring appropriate productivity mix

Productivity mix involves the scheduling of staff in accordance with the skills required to perform a task at maximum efficiency. Multiskilled staff are able to perform a variety of tasks and this helps to increase productivity. Performance standards for tasks must be established and, if applicable, time limitations/productivity specified. The setting of performance standards helps to determine what are considered reasonable productivity levels. This in turn assists in scheduling the correct number and type of staff to perform the duties required.

There are two classifications of employees: fixed cost personnel and variable cost personnel. Fixed cost personnel include your managers and, say, the head chef. They are full-time employees whose weekly wages remain the same regardless of the volume of business. Variable cost personnel are the majority of your part-timers and casual employees. During your peak periods you will increase the number of variable cost personnel, and you will decrease their number during quieter periods.

Fig. 11.2 on pages 128–29 provides two examples of room attendant rosters and outlines how the appropriate mix of fixed cost personnel and variable cost personnel is ascertained.

Fig. 11.1

Sales report showing variations in sales volume.

Weekly Sales Volume	Crab Claw Restaurant					
	Mon		**Tues**		**Wed**	
	Food	Beverage	Food	Beverage	Food	Beverage
Lunch $	1560	630	2470	1100	3452	1454
Covers $	40	40	52	52	78	78
Average per head $	39	15.75	47.5	21.15	44.26	18.64
Dinner $	2650	1340	3420	1605	5674	2555
Covers $	65	65	86	86	130	130
Average per head $	40.76	20.61	39.76	18.66	43.65	19.65
Total F/B $	6180		8595		13135	
Averages $ per head	58.86		62.28		63.15	

Weekly $ Food Lunch 25885	Weekly $ Food Dinner 50454
Weekly $ Beverage Lunch 12347	Weekly $ Beverage Dinner 23815
Total $ Lunch 38232	Total $ Dinner 74269
Total $ Covers Lunch 750	Total $ Covers Dinner 1213
Average $ per head Lunch 50.98	Average $ per head Dinner 61.23

Thurs		Fri		Sat		Sun	
Food	Beverage	Food	Beverage	Food	Beverage	Food	Beverage
3211	1960	3387	1423	5455	2350	6350	3430
96	96	104	104	175	175	205	205
33.45	20.41	32.56	13.68	31.17	13.42	30.97	16.73
5640	2305	13240	5765	14350	7680	5480	2565
127	127	320	320	360	360	125	125
44.41	18.15	41.38	18.01	39.86	21.33	43.84	20.52
13116		23815		29835		17825	
58.82		56.17		55.77		54.01	

	Total Weekly Sales $	112501
	Total Weekly Sales $	112501
	Total Covers $	1963
	Average $ per head	57.31

Fig. 11.2

Comparison of rosters, indicating mix of fixed cost personnel and variable cost personnel.

ROOM ATTENDANT ROSTER

EXAMPLE 1

	Mon	Tue	Wed	Thurs	Fri	Sat	Sun
EXPECTED ROOMS SOLD	40	36	44	48	42	47	42

FULL-TIME EMPLOYEES 7.30am – 4pm (30 minute lunch-break)

	Mon	Tue	Wed	Thurs	Fri	Sat	Sun
David Angelopoulos	RDO	RDO	ON	ON	ON	ON	ON
Jesse Tandy	ON	ON	RDO	RDO	ON	ON	ON
Therese Ng	ON	RDO	RDO	ON	ON	ON	ON
Tom Robbins	ON	ON	ON	ON	RDO	RDO	ON

CASUAL EMPLOYEES

	Mon	Tue	Wed	Thurs	Fri	Sat	Sun
Jenny Gold	800–1200	800–1300	RDO	RDO	800–1200	800–1200	RDO
Katie Wong	RDO	RDO	800–1200	800–1200	800–1100	800–1200	RDO
Bill Murray	RDO	800–1300	800–1200	800–1100	RDO	RDO	RDO

This roster is based on a 50-room hotel where it takes approximately 40 minutes for one attendant to clean one room. It is important to note that the roster is based on the occupancy figures from the previous night, i.e. the number of dirty rooms to be cleaned the following day. For example, when we look at Monday's roster, we are actually looking at the number of dirty rooms that need to be cleaned from Sunday night's occupancy. The number of dirty rooms on Monday morning is 42. Full-time attendants work a 480-minute shift (8 x 60 minutes). Therefore, if we divide 480 minutes by 40 minutes, it means that 12 rooms need to be cleaned by each full-time room attendant rostered on. If we roster on three full-time staff, they can clean 36 of the 42 dirty rooms. That leaves six rooms that still need to be cleaned — 6 rooms x 40 minutes = 240 minutes ÷ 60 minutes = 4 hours of labour to be rostered. Jenny Gold, our casual room attendant, has been rostered on to clean the remaining six dirty rooms. It is important to note that rooms where the guests are staying again for the night will take less time to clean than if the guests were checking out.

ROOM ATTENDANT ROSTER

EXAMPLE 2

	Mon	Tue	Wed	Thurs	Fri	Sat	Sun
EXPECTED ROOMS SOLD	40	36	44	48	26	28	24

FULL-TIME EMPLOYEES

	Mon	Tue	Wed	Thurs	Fri	Sat	Sun
David Angelopoulos	RDO	RDO	ON	ON	ON	ON	ON
Jesse Tandy	ON	ON	RDO	RDO	ON	ON	ON

PERMANENT PART-TIME (half-hour break for lunch)

	Mon	Tue	Wed	Thurs	Fri	Sat	Sun
Therese Ng	RDO	800–1300	800–1200	800–1430	800–1200	RDO	RDO
Tom Robbins	RDO	800–1300	800–1200	800–1430	800–1200	RDO	RDO

CASUAL EMPLOYEES

	Mon	Tue	Wed	Thurs	Fri	Sat	Sun
Jenny Gold	800–1200	800–1200	RDO	800–1200	800–1200	RDO	RDO
Katie Wong	RDO	RDO	800–1200	800–1200	800–1200	RDO	800–1100
Bill Murray	800–1200	800–1200	800–1200	800–1100	RDO	RDO	RDO

This example has the same mid-week occupancy levels as example 1, however the weekend occupancy in example 2 declines quite dramatically. This may be due to the type of client being targeted: the hotel in example 2 may target corporate business people primarily so the weekends will be consistently quieter. In example 2, it is more cost effective to employ fewer full-time staff and more casual and/or permanent part-time staff. This way, there will be the flexibility to roster staff for less than an eight-hour shift when necessary.

QUESTIONS

1 *Will management be able to cover the shifts when staff take their annual leave?*

2 *If a staff member called in sick at the last minute, would management be able to cover the shifts?*

Considering staff needs

As many tourism and hospitality establishments are open seven days a week, 24 hours a day, working hours for most jobs vary considerably. However, it is important to achieve continuity wherever possible as shiftwork can be mentally and physically exhausting and the lack of time spent with family and friends can eventually take its toll.

It is in your best interests, as a supervisor, to be fair and considerate when scheduling your staff since a happy worker is generally a better worker.

The following guidelines may prove useful in your role as supervisor:

- Explain policies and procedures upon commencement of employment so that if, for example, a staff member requests time off or annual leave they are aware of their entitlement.
- Make a copy of the relevant award or agreement available to the employee.
- Give employees their schedules at least two weeks in advance.
- Although not always possible, two consecutive rostered days off enables an employee to enjoy a longer rest period.
- Balance day shifts, evening shifts and night shifts within a rotating roster. It is a fairer approach than giving one employee all evenings or all nights. It may be that your staff prefer particular shifts owing to other commitments, however it is important that they are prepared to be flexible when necessary.
- Try to develop rotating rosters because they allow each full-time employee to enjoy at least one weekend day off every few weeks.
- Allow adequate breaks between shifts. Of particular concern are back-to-back shifts where staff members work an evening shift and are then rostered to work the following day shift.

Maintaining staff records

It is advisable to keep copies of your past staff schedules on file. This information is useful in dealing with enquiries or complaints as they arise. For example, if a guest should complain, it is easy to ascertain which staff were on duty at the time if appropriate records have been kept.

Schedules can also be compared against time sheets when investigating wage cost percentages. However, sophisticated computer software systems are now of great assistance in the management of labour costs. Swipe cards allow the computer to record when employees arrive and leave and also to record when staff change sections during their shifts. This ensures that labour costs are allocated to the appropriate department.

The following request forms should be made available to staff members and filed once action has been taken:

- annual leave
- leave without pay
- long service leave
- bereavement leave
- change of roster
- maternity/adoption leave.

Sickness and accident forms should also be completed and filed.

Monitoring labour costs

One of the most difficult issues facing frontline managers in tourism and hospitality operations is staff turnover. High staff turnover usually means that more staff need training, and this increases labour costs substantially. If casual staff are not valued by management they will quit, creating a cycle of dissatisfaction, poor morale, slow service and high staff turnover. While labour costs can be reduced by using flexible staff, these savings will only be apparent in the long term if casual staff are treated fairly by management.

One large fast food operation directed its managers to save 20 cents per hour on labour costs. This seems a small amount, but it saved enormous sums of money for the organisation as a whole. It is

Fig. 11.3

Variance between projected and actual wages costs for a housekeeping department.

	Monday	Tuesday	Wednesday	Thursday	Friday	Saturday	Sunday	Total Hours	Total $	
Total Labour $ projected	1536.15	1605.45	1570.80	1640.10	1640.10	2599.50	3031.50		13623.60	Target $ ph 13.73
Rostered Hours	133	139	136	142	142	150	150	992		
Daily $ per hour	11.55	11.55	11.55	11.55	11.55	17.33	20.21			
Actual hours worked	133	153	136	141	142	150	167	1022		
Actual Total Labour $	1536.15	1767.15	1570.80	1628.55	1640.10	2599.50	3375.07		14117.32	Actual $ph 13.81
							Variance		$ 493.72	$0.08

Comment: Staff in training on Tuesday; busy period on Sunday due to large number of walk-ins on Saturday night.

a real challenge for a manager to be questioned every time his or her labour costs are 30 cents higher per hour than the store in the next suburb.

Fig. 11.3 illustrates a variance between predicted and actual wages costs for a housekeeping department. This variance would have to be explained by the supervisor. If actual wages costs were below forecast, this would be regarded very favourably.

Decisions regarding staff scheduling have broad ramifications, and readers would be well advised to review the chapter on decision-making and problem-solving before preparing a staff roster.

Discussion questions

1 *How is an industrial award relevant to staff scheduling?*
2 *If you were in charge of staff working shifts, what factors would you consider when preparing their rosters?*
3 *Describe some of the reports that can be used to predict the number of staff required.*

Case study

Jill has been promoted to the position of supervisor. One of her new duties includes the scheduling of staff. The restaurant is open seven days a week from 6.00 am till midnight. Many of the staff have been complaining about the inconsistency in scheduling in the past. The major problems seem to be that the previous supervisor had 'favourites', that the rosters were not fair and that staff were only given a day's notice as to whether or not they were working. The staff say that a lot of the time there was not enough staff on during busy periods and at other times they were standing around trying to look busy.

What planning strategies can Jill use to resolve the past problems involved with scheduling? How can she improve the scheduling system so that the staff will feel that they are being treated with fairness and consideration?

SUMMARY

This chapter has dealt with the complex issue of staff scheduling. First-class service and comfortable working conditions are easy to achieve if there is no limit on staff numbers. However, the reality is that labour costs are higher in Australia than in almost any other country in the world, and profitability is closely related to labour cost. Supervisors are therefore faced with considerable pressure in relation to staffing, both from management and from staff. Balancing the two, and also meeting the demand of customers for fast and friendly service, is one of the most difficult challenges confronting anyone responsible for scheduling of staff.

CHAPTER TWELVE

policies and
procedures

WHEN I WAS ON OVERSEAS ASSIGNMENT I HAD A MOST INTERESTING experience involving implementing company policy. We had a policy which allowed for five days bereavement leave for our staff. An employee of mine had been off work in June because his father had died. We were most sympathetic and sent him off to arrange the funeral and see to his father's affairs. I was stunned when he came back to me the following year to ask for more leave because his father had died. I was most taken aback by this and because of language and communication problems I took the employee to Human Resources to sort out the matter. I assumed that he was using his father's death as a ploy to get leave whenever he asked for it, or that perhaps he had a family crisis that he did not wish to discuss. As it turned out, I discovered that in his traditional family aunts and uncles were treated as mothers and fathers. There was actually no word for 'uncle' or 'aunt' in his language. In his close-knit extended family it was quite possible for more than one mother or father to die. This made it extremely difficult since our corporate policy was five days leave for death in the immediate family.

One of the most important roles of the supervisor is to monitor the implementation of company policies and standard operating procedures. Some organisations have more clearly defined policies and procedures than others. In a small business, for example, arrangements for bereavement leave would be handled on an individual basis. In larger organisations, employee entitlements to all forms of leave would be fully documented.

On completion of this chapter you should be able to:

- **define establishment policy and establishment procedures**
- **explain why policies and procedures are needed**
- **describe the methods used to disseminate policies**
- **describe the methods used to monitor and maintain policies**
- **list relevant legislation and policies which a supervisor should monitor.**

What is an establishment policy?

A policy is by definition a plan or course of action. An establishment policy is a guide for decision-making in the workplace and should be understood by those which the policy affects.

Policies should help to create awareness and to establish systems. For example, executive management might establish a financial policy that employees must obtain approval for all purchases over $200. This policy would specifically state the authority given to supervisors in regard to purchasing and supervisors would know that they were empowered to make purchases within the policy range ($0–200).

Policies may apply to the entire operation or may be specific to one department only. A policy should be stated simply, in writing, and it should be explained to all persons to whom it applies. A policy should relate to organisational objectives, and it should be realistic and capable of being accomplished. It should also set criteria and outline limitations. Policies should be reviewed periodically as conditions change that may affect progress.

What is an establishment procedure?

Procedures are the steps involved in implementing policy. In the previous example, the procedure for cash purchases under $200 would follow different steps from the procedure for purchases over the $200 limit. Purchases over $200 would be handled by the purchasing department and would entail a purchase requisition form which would have to be signed and approved. The purchasing department would obtain the product, which would then be checked and issued to the department requesting it. There are generally several steps which must be followed if standard procedures are to be complied with. In this example, one of the most obvious of these is obtaining a receipt for the product purchased. This is important for accounting and taxation purposes. It also keeps everyone honest.

In the example of the employee asking for bereavement leave, the policy dictated that the allowance would be five days. The procedure would involve completing a leave form which would be forwarded to the human resources department. The information would then be entered into an employee database and stored with the employee's records.

One organisation that is famous for its standard operating procedures is McDonalds. Each McDonalds restaurant must adhere to standard procedures to the letter to ensure that the product is identical in every outlet. There is no guesswork whatsoever, with cooking times specified to the second. In all organisations that seek this level of consistency, standard operating procedures are extremely detailed. In the travel sector, an important procedure is offering travel insurance to a client. This would be done as follows:

1 Offer travel insurance policy (in some agencies, customers are asked to sign an acknowledgement that they were informed about travel insurance).
2 Ensure that the cover is what the customer wants.
3 Ensure that the policy is valid for the appropriate travel dates and that the customer is eligible.
4 Give customer a copy.
5 Advise customer to take the policy with them when travelling.
6 Explain 24-hour assistance program.
7 Advise customer to report stolen property and retain a copy of the police report.
8 Advise customer that reasonable care with belongings would need to be demonstrated.

Communicating policies and procedures

Communication channels used to relay establishment policies and procedures include induction programs, employee handbooks, training sessions, staff meetings, memorandums and verbal reminders.

Induction programs

New employees are usually told about company policies when they attend a formal induction talk. As an example, new staff would be informed that they must use the employee entrance on arrival and departure.

Employee handbooks

Most large organisations issue employee handbooks. Since the first few days in any job are confusing, it is useful to provide policy and procedural information in a written format. Fire procedures are a good example of items that would be found in all employee handbooks.

Training sessions

The importance of following standard procedures is stressed during training. If the reasons why the procedures exist are explained fully, it is more likely that employees will adhere to them. For example, an employee who is told about an accident in which another staff member had cut his hand when using a glass as an ice-scoop is more likely to use the correct procedure and correct tools for the job.

Staff meetings

Meetings provide an ideal opportunity to reinforce messages about policies and procedures. It may be necessary, for example, to remind employees to pick up litter in passing. Visiting senior personnel who have observed employees walking past litter might have precipitated the need to address this situation.

Memorandums

Another method for reminding staff of policies and procedures is the memo. In one kitchen the chef put a note on the third page of a memo to staff (which was placed on the notice board) that any employee who came to him after having read the first two pages could have an extra day off. Unfortunately none of them did!

Verbal reminders

Supervisors often have to remind staff verbally of the need to follow standard procedures. If a supervisor observed a waiter writing an order on a coaster rather than on the correct form, the supervisor would need to point out the importance of giving accurate and complete information to the kitchen.

Monitoring policies and procedures

The role of the supervisor is to maintain and monitor policy implementation. It is therefore beneficial for supervisors and their staff to be involved in the formulation of policies for approval by management. At the operational level the supervisor often needs to develop procedures in order to determine how policy objectives will be achieved. The aim of establishing procedures is to ensure consistency in the performance of tasks, defining actions and in what sequence they are to be carried out.

Quality management programs provide an excellent method for monitoring policy implementation and for making adjustments to existing policies. Customer feedback is one component of a quality management program, customer complaints providing opportunities to review and improve policies and procedures (see Fig. 12.1).

Fig. 12.1

Cycle for changes to policies and procedures.

Where, for example, a guest in a hotel complains that they have not been served in an outdoor area despite being observed waiting by staff from another department, the relevant policy might be changed to include, for example, 'every customer is your concern'. Procedures could then be put in place for dealing with situations where staff provide services outside their usual domain.

The supervisor must know and understand the organisation's policies as situations will arise daily requiring them to make appropriate and correct decisions based on established policy. The methods that the supervisor may use to monitor policy compliance include supervision of staff behaviour, keeping records, appraising performance, conducting disciplinary interviews and implementing control systems.

In a catering company, the policy might state that staff are to wear a specific uniform including chef's trousers, jacket and neckerchief, as well as appropriate footwear. An employee will be reminded of this policy if she turns up to work wearing sneakers. Similarly, any misconduct in the kitchen which places others in danger could lead to dismissal under company policy. It is essential, therefore, that employees be aware of these policies. Employees who are not aware of the policies, rules and guidelines could claim that a disciplinary action was unfair.

Supervisors and managers are also responsible for implementing, maintaining and controlling policies relating to the following government legislation.

Liquor

This legislation covers the responsible service of alcohol to patrons over the age of 18. Severe penalties are incurred by both service personnel and the licensee if the guidelines are not followed and, ultimately, the licensee could lose his or her liquor license.

Occupational health and safety

These laws are designed to prevent accidents and protect staff, including visiting workers who may be working on the premises at the time of an accident. Reporting of accidents, however minor, and observation of health and safety hazards can go a long way in preventing workplace injuries and ill health. Employers have a responsibility to provide a safe workplace and to ensure that safe work practices are implemented. This responsibility is delegated in part to supervisors who must provide the necessary advice to staff and put in place preventative measures.

Hygiene

Careful food handling to prevent contamination is essential. Supervisors need to ensure, for example, that a cutting board is not used for raw chicken, rinsed and used again for fruit salad. Bacteria from the chicken juices could contaminate the fruit salad. If the fruit salad were then left at room temperature for a long period, this could lead to food poisoning. Part of the supervising chef's role would be to provide different cutting boards for different foods and to supervise food preparation.

Equal employment opportunity

This legislation ensures that everyone gets 'a fair go'. This means that staff must be appointed, trained and promoted on merit. Since frontline managers mostly make the final selection decisions, they must ensure that new employees are appointed in accordance with these guidelines. Promotion also needs to be carried out on merit and favouritism avoided.

Affirmative action

The aim of affirmative action legislation is to provide opportunities for minorities to progress in the workforce. Larger organisations are likely to have an affirmative action program which entails keeping statistics on recruitment and career development.

Sexual harassment

Sexual harassment involves actions which are regarded as unacceptable by the receiver. Very often the perpetrator is more

Fig. 12.2

Staff grievance form.

Staff Grievance Form

Job title: Poker Machine Attendant

Employee name: Phillip Swanson

Department: 'Views'

Nature of grievance: Supervisor had shown favouritism to other staff in allocation of shifts and had encouraged rumours that Phillip had stolen personal belongings of another member of staff. Sexual harassment implied.

Provisions of award/agreement violated: None. Hours of work as per award, however staff member allocated higher than average weekend work.

Supervisor's comment: Denied any knowledge of rumours or favouritism in allocating shifts. Guaranteed more consultation in future. Review end month. Unaware of sexual harassment policy.

Action taken: Harassment policy provided and discussed. Supervisor to meet with Human Resources Manager and employee on 20 October 1998.

Supervisor's name: Candice Strong

Union representative's name: Michael Marchetta

Date: 27 September 1998

Candice Strong   _Phillip Swanson_   _Michael Marchetta_
Supervisor's signature   **Employee's signature**   **Union representative's signature**

Fig. 12.3

Example of company policies and procedures.

SPHC GROUP
PARKROYAL · CENTRA · TRAVELODGE

Licensing Laws

If your job requires you to serve alcohol, please note the following.

Under the Liquor Licensing Act you are liable to penalties for serving minors and should take all possible steps to avoid jeopardising the license of the hotel by refusing the service of liquor to minors. If at all in doubt as to whether or not a given customer is a minor, proof of age must be insisted upon. If proof of age is not provided, liquor must not be served. Call your supervisor, departmental manager or manager on duty if difficulties arise.

Health and Safety — Prevention is best

Fire prevention is the responsibility of every employee. It is up to all of us to minimise the risk of a fire starting. Unfortunately fires do occur and it is vital that we safeguard the lives of ourselves, our co-workers and our guests. Know your emergency procedures, the location of fire fighting equipment and fire exits.

Hygiene Legislation — If you are a food handler

Definition

A food handler is defined as a person whose work, at any time, involves him/her handling and/or service of food or drink and the use of utensils or equipment connected with the service and preparation of food and drink.

Procedure

You must report to your supervisor on these occasions:

1 You develop an illness involving vomiting, diarrhoea, skin rash, septic skin, discharge from eye, ear, nose or any other site.

2 Before commencing work following an illness involving any of the above conditions.

3 On return from a trip abroad, during which an attack of vomiting and/or diarrhoea lasted more than two days.

4 If another member of your household is suffering from vomiting or diarrhoea.

In the case of 2 above, the medical certificate you are required to provide on your return from any sick absence must state that you are fit to work.

Employment Opportunities

When an opening occurs in our hotel, those people already employed who have expressed an interest and have shown that they have the attitude and qualifications necessary to perform the job will be considered before we recruit from outside. Decisions to promote will be based on qualifications, experience, previous job performance, attendance record and the interest shown by the employee through participation in the training opportunities available.

Source: Southern Pacific Hotel Corporation. Reproduced with permission.

senior and the other person involved is reluctant to complain. When they do, the complaint needs to be handled confidentially and recorded on a grievance form such as that illustrated in Fig. 12.2 on page 139. Most organisations have a policy on sexual harassment and guidelines for employees who feel the need to speak up about a situation in which they have been involved.

The extract in Fig. 12.3 of policies from SPHC's Parkroyal Darling Harbour Employee Handbook provides a good illustration of company policy, procedure and compliance with relevant legislation.

Many organisations have guidelines for good practice which are based on their policies. In a tourist information centre, for example, staff would be expected to promote all local attractions and to refuse kickbacks from particular operators for promoting them exclusively!

SUMMARY

Policies are developed to ensure compliance with legislation (such as liquor laws) and to ensure that the organisation runs according to the plans developed by senior management. The development of policies provides an opportunity for management to decide on consistent approaches to a range of situations which occur within an establishment. Procedures are the steps devised to ensure compliance with policy guidelines. They provide the foundation for any successful hospitality operation. The frontline manager's role is to ensure compliance with policy and adherence to standard procedures. Policies and procedures are established for good reasons (for example, safety) and it is crucial that employees know why the steps they are asked to follow are important.

The extent to which policies and procedures are defined depends largely on the size of the organisation. Owners and managers of small operations seldom need them as they are on the premises nearly all the time. Large hotel chains develop policy and operational guidelines at corporate level to ensure consistency, although the level of detail varies as many chains give individual hotels considerable scope for making decisions about their daily operations.

Discussion questions

1 *What do you think is involved in responsible service of alcohol? When would you refuse service?*

2 *Do you support affirmative action programs? Analyse both perspectives and give your own conclusion.*

3 *What is the supervisor's role in relation to food handling?*

4 *Give several examples of situations in which disciplinary action might be necessary.*

5 *If you were opening your own business, what would be your policy in relation to the following:*
   - *arrival for shifts*
   - *notification of illness*
   - *uniform requirements*
   - *leave applications.*

Case study

As the owner/manager of a fish and chips shop, you or your partner have always supervised opening and closing procedures. For this reason they have not been formalised. However, now that you are taking a well-deserved holiday, you need to set down procedures for the person who is filling in for you.

Develop a checklist of procedures for closing the shop at the end of the day. Among other things, remind the person to bank the money and lock the door!

CHAPTER THIRTEEN

written
communication

MANY OF OUR LUNCHTIME ORDERS ARRIVE ON THE FAX MACHINE. This makes planning and workflow much easier. We now have valuable time to prepare food in between serving walk-in customers. In the old days we used to lose a lot of trade when customers saw how many people were waiting. We have a special system for faxed orders, so customers save a lot of time too. We deliver to their offices outside the busy lunch period and this has helped us to even out the business during the day and to employ more full-time staff. We use the fax machine to advertise our updated menus and specials for the day to our regular customers.

This small sandwich business has used modern technology to great effect and in this chapter we will look at further ways of using technology to achieve better written communication in the workplace.

Most frontline employees have highly developed verbal communication skills because they are very experienced in the core area of customer relations. However, once promoted to a management role, new demands are placed on their written communication skills. In an industry in which energy and enthusiasm are communicated verbally, the challenge is to convey this same commitment to efficient, quality service, but this time in writing.

The various formats for written communication include:

- memorandums
- standard business letters
- agendas and minutes of meetings

On completion of this chapter you will be able to:

- **write a short memo**
- **write business letters**
- **prepare a meeting agenda**
- **prepare minutes of a meeting**
- **plan the format of a business report**
- **explain the impact of technology on communication in the workplace.**

- reports
- electronic mail.

As a supervisor or manager, you will disseminate vast amounts of internally and externally transmitted information. You will be the adviser, spokesperson, responder and enlightener. You will be writing to customers and suppliers, designing advertising and dealing with government departments.

You must take into account:

- What has to be done.
- Who is involved.
- What time restraints are applicable.

It is important for a supervisor to recognise when a written message is more appropriate than a verbal one. If an employee constantly receives incomplete and ambiguous verbal information from their supervisor, the employee will lose confidence in the supervisor and this will result in dissatisfaction with the job.

An employee must know exactly what to do. It is therefore essential to ask for feedback to ensure understanding. Written communication is beneficial in instances such as this, as well as in dealings with contractors and suppliers, as proof of agreement or course of action, or as confirmation of orders and discussions.

Inter-office memorandums

A memorandum is a simplified standard form of communicating concise information to other staff members, as illustrated in Fig. 13.1.

Business letters

Considering the following will help in developing your letter-writing skills.

Correct punctuation, spelling and grammar

The above mechanical aspects of writing aid both the writer and the reader, ensuring clarity of expression and understanding. As you can see, it is very difficult to understand what is being communicated in the following sentence: 'The maid service does not disorganise your belongings so please tidy up before room clean commencement to avoid complaints'. Today's technology can assist you with spelling and

Fig. 13.1

Sample inter-office memorandum.

MEMORANDUM

DATE: 17 August 1998

TO: Mr Paul Chambers

FROM: Tina Papa

RE: Monthly Occupational Health and Safety meeting

cc: Kerry Liu
Mitchell Dickson

Our monthly meeting is to be held in the conference room on Level 5 at 2.30 pm on Monday, 25 August 1998.

Please assist by compiling the surveyed information regarding Occupational Health and Safety awareness. If you could present the results in graphic format on the overhead projector, this would help us to understand and analyse the information.

Don't hesitate to drop into my office if you would like to review this before the meeting.

Thank you for your assistance.

word usage, but it can do little to help you with grammar and expression. It is up to the writer's judgement whether these mechanical skills are necessary, however your abilities may be judged unfavourably by your peers and clients if you choose to neglect them.

Appropriate tone

An inexperienced writer should not attempt to sound too business like by using stifling words such as 'herewith' or 'thereafter'. While business letters need to vary in tone from formal to familiar, a natural positive tone will help you to succeed in sounding professional. Flowery words and well-worn sentences such as 'Please do not hesitate to contact me' can be more simply stated as 'Please contact me'. This assists in making your letter reader friendly.

Avoid jargon

When corresponding with a client or interdepartmental manager you need to avoid terminology specific to your department or industry. A client may not understand that table d'hôte means a set priced menu or that a guaranteed reservation means that there will be no refund if the guest does not arrive.

Establish rapport

Unfortunately all correspondence to guests or clients may not be of a pleasant nature. For example, if a regular guest has checked out without paying their bill in full, diplomacy and tact in your written communication is far more effective than a personal attack on the reader.

What's in it for the reader?

A reader does not necessarily want to hear about the 'I' (the writer) and the 'we' (your company) throughout your entire letter. 'I' and 'we' do help to establish a friendly tone but the letter should be structured from the reader's point of view. The 'you' approach helps to guide the reader towards the benefits of reading and/or responding to your correspondence. It may also encourage the reader to take action.

Structure of the letter

First plan out what you want to say in point form, listing all details necessary to make your point. The information should be complete and the purpose of your letter should be clear. Edit and proofread

Fig. 13.2

Standard layout for a business letter.

Commercial Conventions Pty Ltd

888 Commercial Street
SYDNEY NSW 2000
Telephone (02) 9226 4518 Fax (02) 9226 4522 E-mail commcon@cia.com.au

31 August 1998   **(DATE)**

Mr P. McDougall
21A Bakers Road
CHURCH POINT NSW 2105   **(RECEIVER'S ADDRESS — BLOCK STYLE/OPEN PUNCTUATION)**

Dear Mr McDougall   **(SALUTATION)**

Re: Confirmation of your meeting booking

(BODY OF THE LETTER)

Thank you for booking our boardroom for your meeting, starting at 9 am and finishing at 3 pm on 23 August 1998.

Morning refreshments break (10 am): Hot scones with homemade jam and fresh cream, coffee, tea and fresh orange juice.

Lunch (12 noon): Seafood buffet, with Pacific oysters, fresh prawns, smoked Tasmanian salmon, a wide range of salads and a selection of cold meats.

Floor plan: U-shape with seating for 12 people.

Audiovisual equipment: Overhead projector and screen.

I will call you on 9427 6721 to discuss final arrangements the day before your meeting. If you have any questions, please call me.

We have a range of other services available and these are described in the attached brochure.

We look forward to catering for your group.

Yours sincerely

(ALLOW AMPLE SPACE FOR SIGNATURE)

Kate Fowler
Conventions Manager   **(NAME AND POSITION OF SENDER)**

Fig. 13.3

Sample warning letter to an employee.

Prestige Hotel

424 Queen Street
MELBOURNE VIC 3000
Telephone (03) 9246 3452   Facsimile (03) 9246 3453
E-mail prestige@info.com.au

2 September 1998

Mr John Andrews
132 Clarrie Street
ST KILDA VIC 3182

Dear John

This letter is a formal written warning in relation to your unsatisfactory behaviour while driving a guest's Porsche 911 on Monday, 31 August 1998. Several staff members and guests have complained, stating that you were spinning the tyres and driving in a hazardous manner.

If this situation occurs again in the future, it will result in dismissal. It has been noted on your employment record that you have received this warning about joyriding in a guest's car.

A copy of this letter will be attached to your personal file. Please come to my office at 10 am on Monday, 7 September 1998 when you will be requested to sign this letter in the presence of your union representative.

Signed

Ally Schilbach

Ally Schilbach
Human Resources Manager

John Andrews

John Andrews
Employee

Phil Jackson

Phil Jackson
Union
Representative

your letter so it is concise, checking spelling, grammar and punctuation at the same time. Finally, check that the layout and overall presentation is professional.

An example of a business letter is given in Fig. 13.2 on page 147 and an example of a formal written warning to an employee is contained in Fig. 13.3.

Agendas and minutes

An agenda lists issues that will be covered during a meeting. It establishes priorities for discussion and helps to keep the group on track. Ideally, an agenda should be distributed to the various parties prior to a meeting.

Minutes are a written record of discussions at a meeting and the outcome of those discussions. Minutes are distributed to those in attendance and are filed for future reference. They also provide information to absentees on what occurred at the meeting.

The minutes of official meetings involving, for example, legal matters are recorded verbatim, or word for word.

Minutes are generally prepared by a secretary or assistant and should include:

- the name of the organisation
- the place, time and date of the meeting
- whether the meeting is scheduled regularly (weekly, for example)
- a record of those who attended (including the name of the person chairing the meeting)
- a reference to the minutes of the previous meeting (if applicable)
- an account of all reports presented, points raised and agreements reached
- points of action and responsibility
- the time of adjournment
- the date, time and place of the next meeting.

Business reports

Reports are produced in varying formats, ranging from statistical reports containing data in the form of charts, tables and graphs to progress reports, which are based on fact and trace the progression of newly developed ideas, and investigative reports which usually include recommendations. As a supervisor you will need to be able to submit, interpret and respond to various types of reports.

There are essential points to remember when compiling a report:

- It must be simple, clear and concise.
- It must be organised in an appropriate format.
- The report must contain complete, accurate information.
- Sources must be referenced so that information may be verified if necessary.
- Informal reports to co-workers may be worded personally, for example 'I recommend . . .' However, a formal report should be expressed entirely in the third person, 'It is recommended . . .'
- A report must be dated so that it can be matched to a specific financial or business activity period.
- A copy of every report should be photocopied and filed for your reference.

Structuring a report

Reports should include the following:

- cover sheet or title page (including the name of the person who has prepared the report, the recipient's name and the date of completion)
- contents page (see Fig. 13.4)
- list of illustrations (if included)
- report summary or abstract (gives the reader general information about what is in the report — 150–300 words)
- introduction (an opening statement of the facts)
- purpose of the report
- range of the report (what it includes)
- method used for obtaining the information
- the body of the report (divided into sections and sub-sections, using either an alphanumerical or a decimal system, allowing for clarity and ease of cross-referencing (see Fig. 13.5)
- conclusion (a summary of the report findings and conclusions)
- recommendations (which should be clear and specific so that immediate action can be taken)
- bibliography (list of reference sources stating author, title, edition, publisher, place of publication and date published)
- appendix (data, separate to the main body, which helps to support the main ideas and facts)

Fig. 13.4

An example of a Table of Contents for reports.

Contents

		Page
1.	Abstract	1
2.	Introduction	2
3.	Analysis of problem areas	
	3.1 Occupational health and safety — electrical hazards	3
	3.2 Staff training	5
	3.3 Documentation of procedures	10
4.	Conclusion	14
5.	Recommendations	
	5.1 Occupational health and safety awareness	16
	5.2 Training courses	18
	5.3 Procedures manual	20
6.	References	22
7.	Appendix	23

Fig. 13.5

Numbering systems for reports.

Alphanumeric System	Decimal System
I. Conference Menus	1. Conference Menus
A. Refreshments	1.1 Refreshments
B. Luncheon	1.2 Luncheon
C. Dinner	1.3 Dinner
II. Beverage List	2. Beverage List

Fig. 13.6
Sample e-mail.

To: <tim.jones@jones.com.au>
From: <joan.simmons@ARF.com.au>
Subject: Access to e-mail from remote locations
cc:
bcc:
Attached:

Tim
>
I could not reach you on the phone. No doubt you are running around the building as usual.
We will be upgrading the Front Office system on 19th February during the early hours of the morning (1am–5am). Please make arrangements for this and confirm them with me on Wednesday, 3rd.

Thanks.
>
>Joan
>

SUMMARY
Supervisors in tourism and hospitality are required not only to have highly developed verbal skills but also to demonstrate effective written communication skills. Useful points on writing business letters, preparing agendas and minutes of meetings, compiling reports, and sending e-mail and memos have been outlined in this chapter, accompanied by a number of examples.

Electronic mail

Electronic mail (see Fig. 13.6) is a speedy and efficient way to communicate. However, it is important that your messages be brief, if possible, and easy to understand. You should also consider carefully the type of messages you send by this method as there is always a possibility that they could be viewed by someone other than the intended recipient.

Discussion questions

1 *Electronic mail is very useful for sending written messages. It also allows the writer to distribute the message to a large number of recipients with a single keystroke. While this is valuable in some situations, it can be a problem in others. For example, staff could use the e-mail system to advertise a car they have for sale and distribute the message to all staff in the building repeatedly over a period of days. How would you go about telling your staff how to use the e-mail system?*

2 *Now that messages are sent by e-mail, this creates a permanent*

*record of what might previously have been an informal
discussion. Messages can also be copied to others. Explain the
impact of the e-mail system on company politics.*

3   *One senior manager banned all staff below executive level from
sending e-mail to her. Why do you think she did this?*

Case study

One

Joe is a newly recruited supervisor at the Crab Claw Seafood
Restaurant. The manager has received a letter of complaint from a
regular guest and as Joe was the supervisor on duty on the evening
that the guest dined at the restaurant he has been given the
responsibility of responding in writing to the guest.

The guest's letter stated that he and his companions waited over
an hour before their main meal order was taken. The lobster ordered
by three of them was chewy and bland and he felt that they were
frozen and not fresh, as advertised.

What action do you think the writer is seeking? How could you
communicate your findings to the writer without offering excuses or
transferring blame? How could you complete your letter on a positive
note?

Two

You have almost finished renovating a magnificent country home to
offer bed and breakfast and you intend to provide fresh bread every
morning (thanks to your brand new bread-making machine),
homemade jams, freshly ground coffee, locally grown cereals and
fresh cream. In the process of planning your small business operation
you need to develop letterhead, standard booking and confirmation
forms, and advertising material.

Write copy for your promotional material and routine
correspondence. The following are suggestions only — you can be as
creative as you wish with the design and wording of your copy:

- weekend package
- mid-week special package
- booking confirmation
- breakfast menu.

CHAPTER FOURTEEN

quality
management

I WAS AMAZED TO READ THE STORY OF THE 86-YEAR-OLD AMERICAN tourist who was trapped inside a hotel stairwell for three days, missing his grand-daughter's wedding. Apparently the door had been rusted shut by salt air. The poor man wrote several notes and pushed them under the door, pleading with people to let him out. Police were conducting air and ground searches for the missing man while the wedding went ahead. This could not happen in our hotel as safety is an important part of our quality program. Our procedures include checks that would have prevented this incident occurring. Can you imagine what would happen in our building if there was a fire? All our staff are committed to our quality management program and we are all invited to attend quality meetings during work hours.

Quality management programs are designed to check on current systems and procedures and to make relevant improvements. In the above case there is clearly room for improvement in the area of hotel maintenance. Most quality management programs aim to implement such improvements before they lead to situations such as this one which resulted in some bad publicity.

Quality is a product of commitment from management, supervisors and operational level staff. Quality goals need to be specific and obtainable and agreed upon by all concerned. This not only helps to prevent resistance to change but also assists in establishing values and standards that workers can believe in and be committed to. Employees need to feel confident that they can achieve their own personal work performance standards as well as departmental performance standards and goals and, where applicable, divisional objectives.

The organisation, as a whole, must have one unified mission statement. A mission statement is a common sense of purpose within the organisation. An example of a mission statement might be: 'Our aim is to provide visiting tourists with appropriate information to meet their specific requirements. This information should be given promptly, in a friendly and positive manner.' From this mission statement, you can see that a number of systems would need to be put in place to make this happen. For the case study at the end of this chapter, you will be asked to make some recommendations to ensure that quality service is provided in this way.

To ensure that management's quality objectives are reached, employees need to be empowered to carry out procedures that will ensure quality service. Empowerment means that employees are responsible for their decisions and actions. This allows for immediate response to customer needs and leads to improvement in the quality of service. It is essential, however, that employees have the skills and knowledge required to make these decisions.

A worker should also feel confident that there is some room for variation from the established procedures, within reason. Mistakes can be rectified and problems can be solved, creating new and more efficient procedures. Trust and good faith is a result of fair feedback. Praise should be given when performance expectations have been met; constructive criticism should be given when they are not. Quality programs are based on continuous improvement and, for this to occur, organisations need to be responsive to issues of concern. Quality cannot improve in a climate of fear in which staff are reluctant to speak up.

The most commonly asked question from a supervisor is 'How do I get my staff to commit to a quality program?'. It is important that a belief in doing something right the first time is conveyed to staff. During induction, employees need to acquire an understanding of the organisation's quality values in relation to customers, both internal (work team members) and external (clients, guests).

To be able to achieve this commitment and understanding, the following is important:

- Employees must be involved in establishing their own work procedures and performance standards.

- They need a guide for measuring their own performance after procedures and standards have been set. This may come in the form of a self-evaluation sheet or a job appraisal.
- Each task within the department must be internally or externally audited. It is important that the employee understand that it is the process that is being audited not the employee.
- All reviews/audits must be documented as to acceptable performance levels.
- Employees must be involved in any procedural changes or improvements once measurable outcomes have been reviewed.
- Reward systems need to be implemented to encourage quality performance.

Evolution of Total Quality Management

In 1946 the Japanese Union of Scientists and Engineers (JUSE) was established. Their aim was 'to contribute to human prosperity through industrial development, achieved by creating, applying and promoting advanced science and technology'. By the early 1960s, the

Fig. 14.1

Deming's quality improvement cycle.

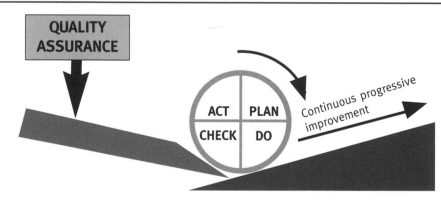

PLAN Collect and analyse information to develop a plan for what needs to be achieved in a given time frame.

DO Do the required actions specified in the plan.

CHECK Check, by gathering information, that the steps taken result in realisation of the plan or otherwise.

ACT Act by standardising the changes which have proven themselves in achieving the plan.

Review the outcomes to ascertain additional opportunities for improvement.

concept of Quality Control was being introduced to the Japanese business community via journals, publications, radio and television, all initiated by JUSE. The idea being expressed was that by including workers in the process of identifying and solving quality problems, it would increase their level of commitment and participation in the quality control of their work. The workers met on a weekly basis to discuss quality issues.

During the early 1940s, W. Edwards Deming, an industrial engineer, had been developing in the United States what was to become known as the 'Deming Cycle': 'Plan, Do, Check and Act (PDCA)' (see Fig. 14.1). The Deming Cycle was based on the realisation that workers were the ones who had actual control of the production process and therefore should be actively involved in the planning, implementation and monitoring of work practices.

JUSE invited Deming to speak at a series of seminars in Japan. By the late 1960s, the majority of Japanese companies had employed Deming's principles, and Japanese manufacturing dramatically improved, as a result of the workers being actively involved in quality procedures.

Dr Joseph M. Juran has also influenced our approach to quality management, with his idea that quality must be based on customer needs and expectations.

Total Quality Management techniques and tools

Technique is the strategy or practice of identifying areas requiring quality improvement. For example, the formation of quality circles to identify, discuss and resolve quality issues is a technique.

Tools are the means by which quality measurements and guidelines are indicated. For example, a control chart showing the variance in the time it takes for guests to receive their meals after they have ordered is a tool. Tools are beneficial in that they help to interpret information and also assist in problem-solving and decision-making.

Control charts

A sample control chart is illustrated in Fig. 14.2. This chart is the graphic representation of measurements taken during the process of meal service in a restaurant. In this example any meal served within the upper control limit (UCL) and the lower control limit (LCL) is

Fig. 14.2

Sample run and control chart.

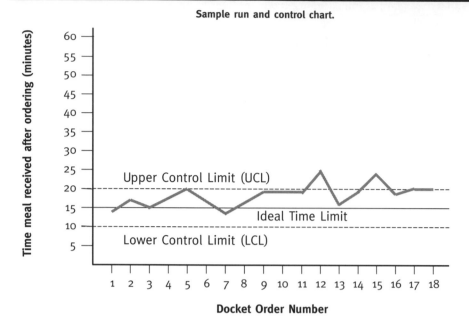

Docket Order Number

considered an acceptable range. The UCL and LCL may have been established as the result of a customer survey. Any variance outside the UCL or LCL is considered unacceptable.

Control charts only demonstrate what actually occurred in a particular situation in a particular time frame, in our example during meal service on one day. The reasons for the variation will still need to be investigated by the quality circle.

Ishikawa diagram (fishbone chart)

Another tool used to identify the causes of quality problems is known as the Ishikawa diagram or fishbone chart. This cause and effect diagram was first developed by Kaoru Ishikawa and is useful in discussion sessions in identifying quality problems and factors that affect the quality process. The problem or defect is graphed at the head of the chart. This is the possible outcome or effect. The backbone branches help to illustrate how various problems within the process affect each other.

An example of a fishbone chart is illustrated in Fig. 14.3.

Flow charts

Also known as input-output charts, flow charts give a visual representation of the flow of procedures involved in a process or task.

Fig. 14.3

The fishbone chart is used to pinpoint the most likely causes of quality problems.

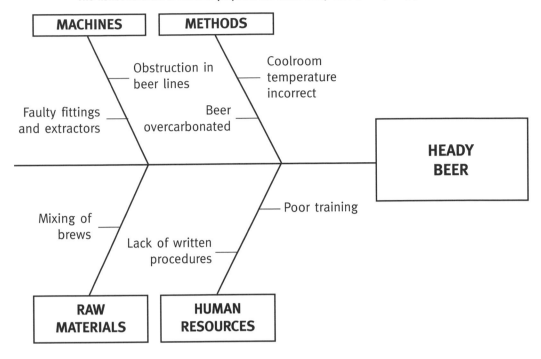

Flow charts are useful in clarifying how a simple process may involve several positions within a number of departments. Flow charts also reinforce the conclusion that the quality of a single good or service is often dependent upon the action of many employees.

Documentation and certification

For businesses to be certified for their quality programs, quality issues must be thoroughly documented.

Firstly, a quality manual must be compiled, containing:

- the organisation's quality mission statement
- a description of quality policies and the target work groups involved
- the name of the standards on which the quality system will be based
- an explanation of how quality systems will be introduced.

This manual acts as a summary of representative quality workplace practices.

Accompanying the quality manual must be a set of procedures

Fig. 14.4

Sample work instruction for handling guest complaints.

Work Instruction

TASK: Handling guest complaints

Performance Procedure

Listen to the guest and do not interrupt. Deal with the guest's feelings first.

Welcome the complaint. Thank the guest for bringing the problem to your attention.

Apologise to the guest for the misunderstanding or inconvenience.

Offer corrective action or solution, seeking agreement from the guest.

Act on action or solution.

Follow up to ensure guest is satisfied.

Inform your manager of the complaint.

JOB TITLE: Guest Services Agent

Quality Standard

All complaints must be handled in a professional manner.

Be courteous and sincere.

Express sincere concern for the inconvenience.

Offer realistic solutions which meet policy guidelines.

Immediately.

Promptly.

Complete a guest incident form promptly.

manuals that are more specific about how the quality program works. The following must be clearly stated:

- objectives of the document
- definition of terminology
- range of procedures (for example, the department and personnel involved in implementing the procedures
- procedural steps (who is involved, what is involved, when it will happen, how it should happen and where it should take place).

Finally, local procedures instructions or work instructions need to be documented. These contain specific performance procedures and standards to be used as guidelines for the workers performing the specific tasks. For example, detailed instructions, with diagrams or illustrations, might be formulated for the cleaning and maintenance of an espresso machine.

Fig. 14.4 is an example of a work instruction for the task of handling guest complaints. Be sure not to take complaints personally, nor to transfer the blame to your colleagues or the establishment. These are opportunities to provide corrective action and win loyal customers.

A booklet on Australian and New Zealand standards for the hospitality industry is available from Standards Australia, National Sales Centre. Standards Reference AS/NZS 3905.3.

Discussion questions

1 How would you design procedures to avoid risks to safety such as the one described at the start of the chapter.

2 Is quality associated with the luxury end of the tourism and hospitality market or can you have good quality at the budget end of this market?

3 The Japanese team-based approach to quality works very successfully. Discuss cultural and other factors that have had an impact on the success of team-based approaches in different organisations and in different countries.

4 Some people argue that so much time is spent on quality reports and diagrams that it defeats the quality objective. Time spent in meetings could be spent in getting the job done. Discuss.

Case study

Henry's restaurant has recently lost a lot of regular guests. A new one opened in a nearby suburb three months ago and Henry feels that he has lost patronage as a result. He decides to take a night off from his restaurant to see what could possibly be so good about his competition. Henry's dining experience is exceptional. The staff are efficient and enthusiastic, and the food is superb. He notices that a

SUMMARY

Quality management is a process of continuous improvement. Since frontline staff have direct contact with customers, they are in a unique position to generate ideas on improved methods of operation. These ideas can be implemented only with the support and commitment of all levels of the organisation to supply the best possible products and services. A positive approach to seeking feedback and solving problems is one of the key components of a quality program. The major outcomes of a successful quality management program are customer satisfaction, increased business and higher profits.

guest's questionnaire is presented with the bill and he asks one of the waiters why he likes his job so much? 'It's our commitment to quality', he replies. On the way home, Henry considers having a meeting with his staff about how they might improve their attitude and wonders if conducting a few customer surveys might also help. If he were to take these steps, surely their situation would improve?

Do you think that Henry's ideas will be effective in improving the quality of his restaurant's products and services? What recommendations would you make to Henry to ensure his restaurant's future?

CHAPTER FIFTEEN

occupational health and
safety

ONE OF THE STAFF WORKING AT THE ANIMAL PARK WAS BADLY burned by chemicals. She was a young volunteer who worked there on the weekends. Although management expressed their 'regret' to the family, they said that since she was a volunteer it was not their responsibility and she was not covered by workers' compensation. The parents argued that the management of the park had a duty of care and that safe systems of work and training should be provided for anyone working on the premises, whether paid or not. The case has gone to court.

The main aim of occupational health and safety legislation is to prevent accidents by providing safe workplaces and safe systems of work. This, of course, includes safe use of tools and equipment. The legislation also states that management is responsible for the safety of visiting workers.

Supervisors must ensure that all employees perform their jobs with due care, with safe work practices being a priority. They must evaluate the work environment and put in place measures to prevent accidents. While employers have a legal responsibility to ensure the health and safety of their staff, it is still the employee's duty to take reasonable care of the health and safety of their fellow employees. This message should be an important part of the induction and training processes discussed in Chapter 6.

The tourism and hospitality industry is very diverse when you consider the fixtures, fittings, machinery and equipment involved, and the range of duties performed by staff. It is therefore imperative that health and safety procedures are carefully documented and that

On completion of this chapter you will be able to:

- describe the main features of health and safety legislation
- assemble information relating to health and safety
- identify signs which should be displayed in the workplace
- develop a training plan to convey health and safety information to staff
- use quality circles to identify health and safety issues and recommend preventative strategies.

these procedures are explained during training in each and every task performed. Health and safety is a serious issue which, if ignored, can result in injury or work-related illness or, at the extreme end, fatality.

Frontline managers carry responsibility for the health and safety of their staff. Their main role is to plan, implement and supervise occupational health and safety, and to formulate responses to emergency situations should the preventative measures fail.

Developing an OH&S strategy

All organisations should have a commitment to occupational health and safety, with an emphasis on employee involvement. The objectives of the program should be incorporated in the policy documents of the organisation.

Staff members need to be trained in the policies and procedures

Fig. 15.1

Signage helps to communicate to employees potential hazards in the workplace.

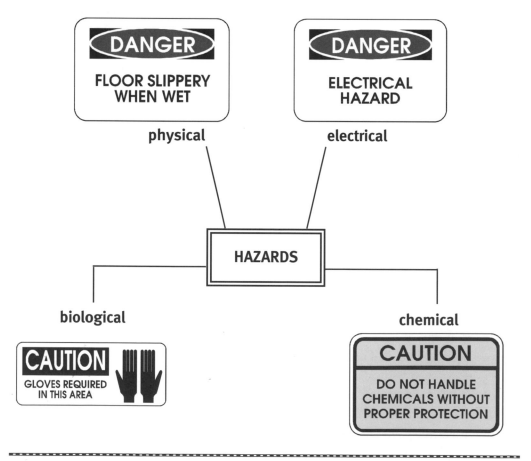

of the OH&S program and should be consulted on a regular basis. The program should be communicated effectively, two-way communication between management and staff being a key issue as it ensures that the program is understood and supported by all employees.

The program can be communicated via the following channels:

- signage (see Fig. 15.1)
- information posted on noticeboards
- newsletters
- meetings and seminars.

Feedback from employees may be through:

- quality circle meetings
- suggestion boxes
- staff meetings.

And the occupational health and safety committee can also communicate and effectively monitor the OH&S program.

Guidelines for accident prevention

Managers and staff need to develop an awareness of occupational health and safety issues in order to understand what can potentially cause an accident or injury. Preventative measures should be taken, including regular safety inspections, regular maintenance and servicing of machinery and equipment, and regular repair of fixtures and fittings. Safety checklists should be introduced. Training of new employees in safe-handling procedures and the correct physical mechanics of performing tasks is another essential part of an OH&S program since new staff face the highest risk of accident or injury.

The necessary documentation for an OH&S program includes hazard report forms, accident investigation forms, and sickness and illness records. Documenting incidents helps to eliminate the chance of the accident or injury occurring again. The report needs to be investigated and analysed, and preventative or corrective measures need to be taken. All recommendations should be implemented immediately and should be reviewed for effectiveness after a period of time.

Methods of hazard identification

Hazards are often categorised by the effect they might have on a person's health or safety. Common categorisation of hazards is outlined below:

- physical hazards (for example, excess noise levels causing headaches and hearing problems)
- electrical or mechanical hazards (for example, electric shock)
- psychological hazards (such as stress causing high blood pressure)
- chemical hazards (resulting in poisoning or allergies, for example)
- biological hazards (resulting in illness, such as food poisoning).

The significance of the hazard is based on a combination of three factors:

- frequency (how often the person is in contact with the hazard)
- duration (how much exposure is required before health is affected)
- severity (the extent of the hazard).

It is also important to consider the attributes of the person who is performing the task. Physical capabilities are a concern when the person performing the task is considered below the established range of what is acceptable, for example a pregnant woman should not be allowed to lift heavy weights. The level of skill or expertise of the person is also relevant. If an employee is not adequately trained in performing a task, then the potential for accident or injury is higher. Similarly, if a procedure becomes automatic because an employee is bored and paying little attention to, for example, safe-handling procedures, there is greater possibility of accident or injury.

Accident reporting

As reporting accidents is a legal requirement, accident report forms or accident registers have to be created and maintained. The following details should be documented:

- name, age, address and occupation of the casualty
- industry in which the casualty is working
- task being performed when the accident occurred
- time and location of the accident
- how the accident occurred
- why the accident occurred.

Fig. 15.2

Example of an accident report form

Injury/Illness Report

Details of the person injured or ill

Surname: Goldsmith   **Given name:** Jeremy

Home Address: 12 Sunny Street, Palm Lake   **State:** Qld   **Postcode:** 4227

Telephone: (07) 5492 9900

Sex: Male   **Date of birth:** 16. 7.1963

Is the person an employee or visitor? Employee

If an employee, please complete the following details

Job title: Bar Attendant   **Department:** Cove Restaurant

Period of employment: 12 months

Occurrence details

Date of injury/illness: 17. 9.1998   **Time of occurrence:** 7.30pm

What was the person doing when injured? Unloading glasses from glasswasher which was overstacked.

Describe the worker's injury or illness: Serious cut to the middle finger of the left hand; copious bleeding.

Details of treatment: Cut required three stitches. Cut was cleaned and bandaged by First Aid Officer on duty before seeing family doctor. Gloves were not in the First Aid kit, increasing the risk of cross-contamination.

Action required

1 OH&S training for all bar and stewarding staff and supervisors by Joseph Choi before 31 October 1998.

2 Poster to be placed above dishwasher.

3 Review procedures for checking First Aid kit.

Name of person reporting injury: Jane West **Position:** Cove Rest. Supervisor

Witness name: John Lucciano, Bar Attendant

Address: 2 Short Street, Palm Lake 4227   **Telephone:** (07) 5492 2785

Information about the injuries should also be recorded and any medical certificates and/or examination reports should be attached.

A sample accident report form is contained in Fig. 15.2 on the previous page.

Occupational health and safety acts

These are State and Territory acts that aim to protect people at their place of work, including self-employed persons, from injury or harm.

Guidelines to the main provisions of general duties (Part 3, Division 1) of the Occupational Health and Safety Act NSW 1983 are summarised below, as an example.

Employer responsibilities

As an employer you must:

- provide adequate training, including detailed instruction and supervision, to ensure a safe and healthy work environment
- provide researched information and testing results in regard to substances used at work
- ensure that all equipment and systems of work are maintained to ensure that they are safe
- establish procedures for handling, storage, safe use and transportation of all equipment and substances
- ensure the work environment is in a safe condition, including safe entrances and exits.

Employers are solely responsible for the financial costs of the above and cannot request an employee to pay for any of the costs that may be involved.

The provisions of the Act also include responsibility for ensuring that the health and safety of visitors to the workplace is not at risk.

Employee responsibility

The following are extracts only from Part 3, Division 1 of the Act that apply to employee responsibility:

'19 **Employees at work to take care of others and to co-operate with employer**

Every employee while at work:

(a)   shall take reasonable care for the health and safety of persons who are at his place of work and who may be affected by his acts or omissions at work, and (b)　shall, as regards any requirement imposed in the interests of health, safety and welfare on his employer or any other person by or under this Act or the associated occupational health and safety legislation, co-operate with him so far as is necessary to enable that requirement to be complied with.

20　Persons not to interfere with or misuse things provided for the health, safety and welfare

A person shall not intentionally or recklessly interfere with or misuse anything provided in the interests of health, safety and welfare in pursuance of this Act or the associated occupational health and safety legislation

21A　Person not to hinder aid to injured worker etc

(1)　A person shall not, by intimidation or by any other act or omission, wilfully hinder or obstruct or attempt to hinder or obstruct:

(a)　the giving or receiving of aid in respect of the illness or injury of a person at work, or

(b)　the doing of any act or thing to avoid or prevent a serious risk to the health or safety of a person at work.

(2)　A person at a place of work shall not refuse any reasonable request:

(a)　for assistance in the giving or receiving of aid in respect of the illness or injury of a person at work at that place of work, or

(b)　for the doing of any act or thing to assist in the avoidance or prevention of a serious risk to the health or safety of a person at work at that place of work.'

Occupational health and safety committees

An occupational health and safety committee should be established at any place of work with more than 20 employees or where the majority of the people employed requests the establishment of such a committee. Sometimes Workcover Authority directs the establishment of such a committee at a place of work.

The OH&S committee performs a number of functions. It monitors measures taken to ensure the health and safety of people at a place of work and investigates health and safety related issues. The committee also makes recommendations for improvements in health and safety in the workplace.

Members of an OH&S committee should be provided with training and support in order to fully exercise their function as a member.

An important provision of the Act relates to unlawful dismissal of an employee. An employee cannot be dismissed or injured or his or her position altered to their detriment if the employee makes a complaint about a matter which he or she considers is not safe or a risk to health.

The recommended composition of an OH&S committee includes representatives from:

- both sexes
- different cultures
- each shift
- varying trades and skills
- each section of the workplace.

The employee committee members must elect one of the employee representatives to be the committee chairperson.

Discussion questions

1   *Employees should not have to worry about health and safety; it is the responsibility of managers to see to it that the workplace is safe. Discuss.*
2   *The limited training of many staff in the tourism and hospitality industry has serious implications for managers responsible for workplace health and safety. Why has this issue of training been allowed to occur?*
3   *Occupational stress is said to be high in the industry for two reasons. Firstly, there is the emotional strain of 'putting on a happy face' in sometimes difficult situations. Secondly, there is the physical and social impact of working shiftwork. Discuss occupational stress in the tourism and hospitality industry and relate it to that in other industries.*

SUMMARY

An important role of the supervisor is responsibility for the health and safety of other employees. In this chapter we have covered the main aspects of health and safety legislation that relate to the tourism and hospitality industry. The importance of planning and involving employees in the development and monitoring of the organisation's occupational health and safety program has been emphasised, as well as the necessity for the implementation of measures to prevent accident or injury. Training of new staff in the OH&S components of all tasks and good communication between employees and management were seen as essential requirements for a successful OH&S program.

Case study

All duty managers in your club have general as well as specific responsibilities. One of your specific responsibilities is occupational health and safety. One of the most serious accidents to have occurred in your workplace was a back injury caused by lifting. The staff member concerned has suffered permanent damage to his spine.

You have been asked to discuss health and safety with a group of staff in their quality circle, and to develop preventative measures and methods of communicating them to other staff. To ensure that awareness of health and safety in your workplace has increased you need also to develop a control system to check compliance with the recommendations.

CHAPTER SIXTEEN

security

On completion of this chapter you will be able to:

- identify security issues relevant to the tourism and hospitality industry
- list and describe legislation which covers security procedures
- list steps to be taken or preventative measures necessary to counteract the above risks
- record security-related incidents
- maintain security records.

I WILL ALWAYS REMEMBER THE MORNING THAT A GUEST ADVISED front office staff that a lady was loading linen into the boot of her car which was parked in front of the fire escape door. When interviewed by security, it was discovered that the woman was in fact a registered guest at the hotel, who had decided to help herself when she discovered an unlocked room attendant's linen store. She had already packed five sets of bed linen, 22 towels and at least 70 tiny bottles of 'complimentary' shampoo. Most amazing of all, she had taken several boxes of toilet paper, too!

Security is an issue for tourism enterprises because they need to protect themselves, while at the same time reducing risks to customers and staff. The above incident of theft — in this instance, by a customer — is an example of security issues that can occur. Customers also need assurance that they are in a safe environment, particularly when travelling far from home.

All employees have a duty of care for customers' and other staff members' safety. All staff should also be trained to look after their employer's interests and to report breaches of such aspects as security. In fact, this is a common law duty of all employees and includes the disclosure of relevant information and the accounting to employers for all monies. Employee awareness of this responsibility to the employer and the customer is the key to safety and security. Once again, these issues need to be stressed during induction and training. Security (including accountability for money) is one of the supervisor's most important control functions. Earlier in this book the management role was described in terms of planning, organising, implementing and controlling. This final chapter has a strong emphasis on the control function of management.

Security involves the provision of an environment for customers which is free from the threat of being personally harmed or having possessions stolen or vandalised. This is particularly relevant to hotels and gaming enterprises, such as casinos and clubs. Security is also concerned with criminal intent to defraud an establishment.

Security liability

Various acts limit liability for providers of accommodation, and include:

- Innkeepers Act 1968 (NSW)
- Carriers and Innkeepers Liability Act 1958 (VIC)
- Liquor Licensing Act 1988 (WA)
- Liquor and Accommodation Act 1990 (TAS)
- Hotelkeepers Act 1981 (NT)
- Innkeepers Liability Act 1902 (ACT).

Specific limited liability legislation no longer applies in Queensland and South Australia.

These acts are concerned with limiting the liability for property damaged or lost on the premises unless it is deposited for safekeeping. The majority of new hotels now provide safety deposit boxes with combination locks within guests' rooms. Notices of limited liability must be displayed within the guest's room as well as at reception. Many convention/function centres include a limited liability policy in their booking contract.

Under common law a guest may make an injury or damages claim against the proprietor of the business if neglect to provide reasonable duty of care can be proven.

Protecting guests and their property

Certain measures need to be taken in the accommodation sector of the industry to ensure the security of guests and their property.

Physical precautions

Physical precautions include:

- provision of self-locking doors with safety chains and/or peep holes in guest rooms
- installation of adequate locking systems on all balcony doors and windows

- provision of a key deposit box on all room attendants' trolleys for the depositing of guests' keys left in the rooms after check-out.

Procedural precautions

The following procedures should also be put in place:

- If a room key has been reported stolen or missing, the barrel of the lock needs to be replaced immediately and the guest issued with a new key (in some cases a charge to the guest may be applicable).
- Staff members who need access to a guest's room must never leave the door open while the room is unattended.
- Room attendants should be careful to close the entrance door when cleaning adjoining rooms within the guest's suite.
- All personnel should be made aware during training that they must not open guests' rooms to strangers. The person must be able to prove that they have been registered in the room at front office.
- Front office staff must never give out keys to a room until the guest has produced identification to show that they are the guest registered for that room.
- Room attendants must never leave their keys on trolleys. Keys should be physically attached to the room attendant's belt.

As visitors to a different country or city, your guests may not be aware of security precautions that they need to take themselves. Front office staff should advise guests of the following security precautions:

- They should not leave keys unattended and should close the entrance door to their room at all times, even when the room is occupied.
- They should not carry large amounts of cash.
- They should leave passports and other valuable documents with the hotel for safekeeping whenever possible.
- They should not leave handbags, briefcases and luggage unattended.
- They should not leave valuables in their car, and their car should be locked when unattended.

Exercising discretion

Employees must never disclose guest room numbers to other guests, including during phone enquiries. The guest's room number must never be stated aloud as prying ears may be listening. Guests and their activities should not be discussed with the general public or other guests. Discussion between staff members concerning guests should be restricted to information needed to perform a duty of work.

Ensuring security of establishment and staff property

The security of the establishment may be the combined responsibility of in-house personnel and an externally contracted security company. Security devices such as surveillance cameras and alarm systems, combined with regular patrols and inspections of all areas, assist in the process of maintaining a safe environment. Photo identification tags as part of the staff uniform help to prevent strangers from gaining access to restricted areas. Coded doors also assist in limiting access to restricted staff areas such as storerooms and cash control rooms. Staff should be provided with lockers to store their personal belongings.

All contractors and tradespersons should be supervised and subject to general inspections.

Many establishments also limit staff entrance and exits to the building, allowing identification checks and random bag inspections, to deter theft by staff. Staff need to be advised that searches of personal belongings may be required when leaving the building. However, some staff find imaginative ways to circumvent searches, a group in one hotel arranging to remove the silverware from the building through the garbage disposal system!

Keys and key-coded cards

Controlling access is one of the highest priorities of security. Staff need access to certain areas to perform their duties, but in the carrying out of these duties strict security procedures must be adhered to.

Access to guest rooms by room attendants during daily cleaning is one of the main concerns of hotel security. Each room attendant must be made accountable for keys issued. The issuing of keys must also be traceable, which is why key or keycard logbooks need to be maintained. The logbook details which keys or cards have been issued and to whom, and also records sign-in and sign-out times and dates in column format.

Keys are usually classified as:

- dedicated keys (for one lock only, for example a guest's room key)
- submasters (open all locks in a specific area, for example floor keys for room attendants)
- master (departmental key which opens all rooms within a division, for example the food and beverage department key which is issued to the food and beverage manager)
- grandmaster (opens all doors and locks in the establishment, usually restricted to the security manager, general manager and duty manager).

Technological advancement has increased the accountability of employees as coded key cards allow the recording of who has accessed a lock at any given time. Cards also increase guest room security as the door-lock code is changed after each guest departs.

Cash handling procedures

Your staff need to be trained in specific cash security procedures. Cash should never be left unattended. Money must be counted in a safe, secure area, and banking routines should be varied so that there is no predictability in the movement of cash takings. Floats must be counted and signed in and out in the presence of a witness, and then recorded in a float logbook.

Following procedures for lost and found property

It is important that employees are trained in the procedures to follow with lost property in accordance with your in-house policy. In hotels, the general procedure is for all items left in guests' rooms to be handed in to the housekeeping department. These items are recorded and stored for a period of time to allow guests the opportunity to claim the goods. Valuable items are passed directly to the security department for safekeeping until the owner has been contacted. Items left in restaurants, bars and other areas of the establishment are passed on to security for storage. Hotel policy may be to wait for the guest to make contact, for reasons of discretion.

Emergency procedures

Security personnel should be professionally trained in emergency procedures and they should be one of your initial contacts should an emergency occur. As the security and welfare of all customers, visitors and staff members is the concern of everyone, all employees should be trained in standard emergency procedures during their induction period. Emergency contact numbers should be displayed on all phone extensions, preferably in several languages if the workplace is a multilingual one.

Fig. 16.1

Recommended evacuation procedure for hotels. New South Wales Fire Brigades.

Emergency Actions

1 Immediately notify the Emergency Service/s required:

- Fire Brigade
- Police
- Ambulance

by dialling 'OOO', or 'O' — 'OOO' in the case of PABX systems. When answered nominate the Emergency Service required.

INFORMATION REQUIRED

Name of the hotel

Street name and number

Suburb

Nearest cross street and prominent landmark

Nature of the incident, for example fire, explosion, etc

State whether or not persons are injured or trapped.

2 Evacuate immediate area to a safe position — account for all staff and guests:

a) Should the incident be of a minor nature, evacuation may only be essential in the immediate area.

b) In the event of a major incident, evacuation of the entire premises and adjacent properties may be necessary.

NOTE: Evacuation in relation to smoke, chemical spillage and gas escape will be governed by existing conditions at the time of the incident. Wind direction and topography are important factors when considering safe areas.

c) Evacuation should take place through the nearest and safest available exit, either normal or alternate routes. All doors should be closed if possible by the last person(s) exiting to contain the fire and smoke to its area of origin.

d) Do not use lifts in case of fire, or emergency. Bring all lifts to the ground floor and isolate.

e) When descending fire stairs with large groups of people, the stairs can become claustrophobic for the evacuees.
Other problems that may be encountered in the stairs include:
- mobility-impaired people trying to descend stairs
- evacuees panicking, stampeding down the stairs
- evacuees awaiting rescue from the roof found trapped at the top of the stairs.

f) Once clear of the building, persons should proceed directly to the predesignated assembly area. No person should be permitted to return to the inside until authorised by the emergency authority.

3 Without endangering personal safety:

a) If possible, and only if safe to do so, nominated staff should attempt to control/extinguish the fire with installed fire fighting equipment (remember evacuation is top priority).

b) Should the fire escalate or threaten personal safety, immediately evacuate the area, closing doors and windows if possible to confine the fire and smoke to its area of origin.
NOTE: It is emphasised that fire fighting measures by staff with installed equipment (portable extinguishers and hose reels) is purely a **'first aid measure'** pending arrival of the Fire Brigades. Should any doubt exist as to the safety of personnel, they should be immediately withdrawn.

4 Have detailed a responsible person to meet emergency services and direct them to the incident area, and also give information regarding the evacuation, injured persons, missing persons, together with last-known whereabouts, if still believed to be within the danger area.

5 Technical assistance:
Have on stand-by technical personnel (for example, engineers) who may be able to give assistance to emergency personnel.

a) Engineering staff who can advise on plant isolation, shut-down procedure and installed fire protection.

Emergency procedures should be designed for the following situations: bomb threats, gas leaks, chemical spills, armed hold-ups and fire.

Fig. 16.1 contains an extract from the New South Wales Fire Brigades' Community Safety Training Services booklet outlining guidelines for evacuation procedures from a hotel.

The most common emergency situation is fire. Even in the

Fig. 16.2

Types of fire extinguishers and their uses. New South Wales Fire Brigades.

Indicator	Class of Fire		A	B	C	(E)	F
FIRE EXTINGUISHER	Type of Fire		Ordinary combustibles (wood, paper, plastics, etc.)	Flammable and combustible liquids	Flammable gases	Fire involving energized electrical equipment	Fire involving cooking oils and fats
Post 1995 / Pre 1995	Identifying Colours	Type of Extinguisher	Extinguisher Suitability				
		WATER	YES Most suitable	NO	NO	NO	NO
		WET CHEMICAL	YES	NO	NO	NO	YES Most suitable
		ALCOHOL RESISTANT FOAM	YES	YES Most suitable for alcohol fires	NO	NO	NO
		AFFF TYPE FOAM	YES	YES Most suitable except for alcohol fires	NO	NO	NO
		AB(E) DRY CHEMICAL POWDER	YES	YES	YES	YES	NO
		B(E) DRY CHEMICAL POWDER	NO	YES	YES	YES	YES
		CARBON DIOXIDE (CO2)	YES*	YES	NO	YES	YES
		VAPOURIZING LIQUID (fumes may be dangerous in confined spaces)	YES*	YES 5 KG ONLY	YES	YES	NO

NOTE: As from 31 December 1995 Halon extinguishers ceased to be legal extinguishers. For Class 'D' fires (involving combustible metals), use special purpose extinguishers only.
* Carbon dioxide and vapourising liquid extinguishers are not suitable for deep-seated smouldering A class fires.

smallest tourism operation, fire is a serious threat. Fires can break out in snack shops, on boat cruises, or on camping tours. So, whether you run a small bed and breakfast or a large motel, all staff should know how to use a fire extinguisher and which one to use, depending on the situation. Checking that extinguishers are of the appropriate type and in working order is part of the control process. Various types of fire extinguishers and their uses are illustrated in Fig. 16.2 on page 179.

As you can see, many supervisor's and manager's duties are directed towards the prevention of accidents and emergencies. All supervisors should be certified in First Aid to ensure that reasonable care will be taken and correct First Aid procedures carried out during all shifts and in emergencies.

Preventing fraud

Many methods of payment are acceptable in travel agencies, hotels, clubs and restaurants, most of which are open to fraud unless approved procedures are followed.

Staff should be trained in the procedures for pre-authorising and authorising credit card sales. All cards should be checked against the warning bulletins issued by credit card companies in case they have been cancelled or stolen. Some credit card companies offer a reward for the seizure of stolen credit cards.

Travellers cheques need to be countersigned in the presence of a cashier and identification details recorded, a passport being the recommended means of identification. Cash must be checked to ensure it is not counterfeit.

Personal cheques are not usually accepted unless prior arrangements have been made with management, or a contract is in place with a cheque authorisation company.

If a company or guest requests to charge their expenses to the company on a credit basis, the company must have a formally approved credit account with the establishment. The company must also send a letter authorising the charges. The letter must state the customer's name, what is allowed to be charged to the company and what the customer must pay themselves, and in the case of accommodation, arrival date, departure date and room type. The letter must be on company letterhead with an authorised signature.

Travel agent vouchers must be checked for authenticity. The numbers should be recorded at the time of reservation and noted on check-in when presented by the guest.

Fig. 16.3

An example of a Guest Incident Form.

Guest Incident Form

Guest name(s): _Smithhaven, Palms, Petrov_

Guest room number(s): _1201, 1202_

Location of incident: _Guest rooms_

Date of incident: _25 August 1998_

Nature of incident: _Duty Manager responded to complaints of loud music and crashing noises. Band members had caused considerable damage to furnishings and fabrics, had stained the carpet and broken the shower screen._

Persons involved: _Jackie Taylor, Duty Manager_

Tony Allan, Turndown Attendant

Carry Silveus, Security Officer

Witnesses:

Does an accident report need to be completed? _No_

Did hotel security or emergency services become involved? _Yes_

If yes, please state details: _Carry was called to the room immediately._

Action taken/outcome: _Police were called and guests evicted after paying for damages._

Jackie Taylor
Supervisor's signature

Tony Allan
Witness's signature

Carry Silveus
Security signature

Recording security incidents

A breach of security needs to be reported to the security department. Depending on the degree of seriousness and urgency, police assistance may be required.

Formal documentation not only assists in the accurate recording of the details of the incident but may also be required as legal evidence in some cases. Factual information, such as the date, time, location and the people involved, including staff members, needs to be recorded. If a person cannot be identified, a description needs to be noted. Security incident forms should preferably be signed by a witness. Evidence from the scene of the incident should not be tampered with or discarded.

An example of a guest incident form is given in Fig. 16.3 on the previous page.

Discussion questions

1 *Hold-ups are a concern for most tourism operations. How can supervisors best train staff to deal with this type of situation?*
2 *Give examples of the types of security incident that could lead to the police being called.*
3 *One major security incident involving a tourist could affect the whole tourism market and damage the economy. Discuss.*

Case study

The Royal Majestic Hotel has been open for just three months. The business is running well, guest numbers are more than satisfactory, and both management and staff seem very happy. However there is one major concern troubling the general manager. The first stocktake of hotel supplies has just been completed. It appears that stock is being absorbed at a much higher level than can be accounted for. A lot of crockery and glassware is missing from the functions department, toiletries and linen are missing from housekeeping, and the past two monthly stocktakes of food and beverage stock has been out. This is costing the business a small fortune and must be investigated immediately.

How can these matters be analysed effectively and the problems solved? What security devices can you think of that may act as a crime deterrent?

SUMMARY

In this chapter we have covered the important issue of security, particularly as it relates to the tourism and hospitality industry. While in large establishments, security is generally the responsibility of a special department, often in conjunction with an external security company, all employees have a duty of care for customers and their fellow staff members. Supervisors and other staff members have a responsibility for protecting guests from threats to their personal safety and their property, as well as for the security of the establishment and staff property. Guidelines for successfully ensuring the safety of all involved have been outlined, as well as steps to be taken in the event of emergencies.

integrated
case study

In this case study, you will be asked to make a range of decisions to show how you would:

- monitor and improve workplace operations to improve customer service
- plan and organise workflow to increase efficiency and profitability
- manage staff to increase job satisfaction and productivity.

If you are already working in a tourism or hospitality environment, you may prefer to make similar decisions for your own workplace.

Your name is Jackie Brown. When your promotion was first announced a week ago, you were delighted with your appointment to the role of supervisor since this meant that you were now on the first rung of the management ladder. Little did you realise how tough it would be. At the time you thought, 'This is my opportunity to implement all the changes I had such good ideas about when I was "just" an employee. Now for the first time I will be making decisions and asking people to follow my instructions.'

Where you work there are seven full-time employees and a number of casuals, depending on the season and various other factors. The full-time staff are shown in the organisational chart on the following page. The business is owned and run by Stephan who is artistic and temperamental, but adored by both customers and staff.

Organisational chart of establishment.

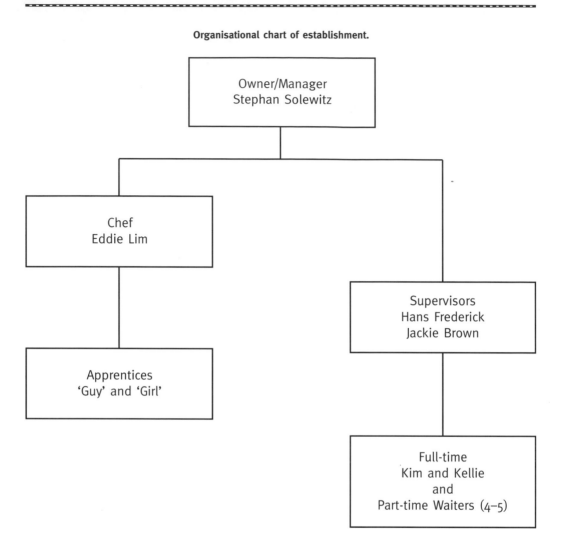

Fortunately your personal relationship with Stephan has cooled enough not to compromise you in your new role.

Your enthusiasm for the job is soon dampened when Stephan calls you in to the office with Eddie and breaks the news that the bank is recommending closing because the restaurant is not profitable, despite the fact that it is busy during peak times. According to Stephan, the Bank Manager has said that staff costs are too high a proportion of sales. This upsets you because you know that the level of service offered is the reason why most customers come back.

You are, however, not as upset as Eddie, who throws his toys out of the cot when Stephan tells him that the Bank Manager has said that such a small business does not need qualified kitchen staff. Eddie is a superb chef, trained in French, Vietnamese and Thai cooking. He is also doing a wonderful job with the two apprentices who are indentured to the restaurant to complete their training. Both 'Guy' and 'Girl' have won medals at the skills Olympics. 'Guy' is a third year apprentice and 'Girl' is a second year apprentice. The Bank Manager has also said that the kitchen brigade should be replaced by a cook and a kitchen hand.

Your concern for Eddie, who storms out without discussing the issue further, evaporates when Stephan suggests that all full-time waiting staff should be replaced by part-timers. This will mean that your friends, Kim and Kellie, will no longer enjoy any job security and will probably leave you high and dry.

Before you get too worked up, Stephan goes out the back where Eddie is having a cigarette and a sulk, and calls him back in to try to salvage the situation. He says that staff costs will have to be trimmed, back and front of house. Both you and Eddie have to take your old rosters and a copy of the award and work out more efficient staffing approaches. He asks you to look at ways in which the number of customers served during peak periods can be increased — to look, in fact, for any kind of efficiency. He also asks you to think about ways in which morale and productivity can be increased — what an ask! Finally, the light at the end of the tunnel is his suggestion that you and Eddie work together on plans to add catering for surrounding office blocks to the restaurant's services.

Stephan reassures you that big changes do not have to occur right away and that the Bank Manager can be appeased if a decrease in labour cost is demonstrated.

You and Eddie need to go away and come back with a plan to:

- monitor and improve workplace operations to improve customer service
- plan and organise workflow to increase efficiency and profitability
- manage staff to increase job satisfaction and productivity.

Go to it!

Bibliography

Andrews, D. & Andrews, W. *Business Communications*. Macmillan, New York, 1988.

Blake, R. R. & Mouton, J. S. 'Managerial Facades'. *Advanced Management Journal*, July 1966, p. 31.

Blake, R. & Mouton, J. *The New Managerial Grid*. Gulf Publishing, Houston, 1978.

Dittmer, R. & Griffin, G. *Principles of Food, Beverage and Labour Cost Controls*. Van Nostrand Reinhold, New York, 1994.

Drummond, K. *Staffing Your Foodservice Operation*. Van Nostrand Reinhold, New York, 1991.

Educational Institute of the American Hotel and Motel Association. *Security Key Control and Guest Privacy*. Educational Institute of the American Hotel and Motel Association, Michigan, 1987.

Ellis, R. and the Security Committee of the American Hotel and Motel Association. *Hospitality Management Library: Security*. Educational Institute of the American Hotel and Motel Association, Michigan, 1986.

Eunson, B. *Writing Skills*. John Wiley & Sons, Brisbane, 1994.

Fiedler, R. & Chemers, M. *Leadership and Effective Management*. Scott Foresman and Company, New York, 1974.

Geffner, A. *Business Letters the Easy Way*. Barron's Educational Series Inc., New York, 1991.

George, C. & Cole, K. *Supervision in Action*. Prentice Hall, New York, 1992.

Hersey, P. & Blanchard, K. *Management of Organization Behavior* (3rd ed.). Prentice Hall, Englewood Cliffs, N.J., 1977.

Herzberg, F., Mausner, B. & Synderman, B. *The Motivation to Work*. John Wiley & Sons, New York, 1959.

How Tourism Labour Markets Work, Research Paper No. 1, Commonwealth Department of Tourism. Australian Government Printing Service, Canberra, 1995.

Jones, P. & Merricks, P. *The Management of Food Service Operations*. Hospitality Press, Melbourne, 1995.

Juran, J. *Juran's Quality Control Handbook* (4th ed.). McGraw Hill, New York, 1998.

Katz, Robert L. 'Skills of an Effective Administrator'. *Harvard Business Review* 52, 5, Sept. 1974.

Keiser, J. *Controlling and Analyzing Costs in the Food Service Operations*. Macmillan, New York, 1989.

Kohr, R. *Accident Prevention for Hotels, Motels and Restaurants*. Van Nostrand Reinhold, New York, 1991.

Maslow, Abraham. *Motivation and Personality*. Harper & Rowe, New York, 1954.

Miller, J., Porter, M. & Drummond, K. *Supervision in the Hospitality Industry* (2nd ed.). John Wiley, New York, 1992.

Mintzberg, H. *The Nature of Managerial Work*. Prentice Hall, Englewood Cliffs, N.J., 1973.

Stoner, J., Collins, R. & Yetton, P. *Management in Australia*, Prentice Hall, Sydney, 1985.

Tourism Accommodation Report No. 50, April 1996. Australian Government Printing Service, Melbourne, 1996.

Tourism Forecast, June and December 1997, June 1998. Office of National Tourism, Canberra.

Tourism Workforce 2020. Tourism Training Australia, 1996. Copyright Australian National Training Authority.

Vroom, V. H. *Work & Motivation*. John Wiley & Sons, New York, 1964.

Wheatley, D. *Report Writing*, Penguin, England, 1988.

Index